John Stuart Blackie

Lays and Legends of Ancient Greece

John Stuart Blackie

Lays and Legends of Ancient Greece

ISBN/EAN: 9783337163563

Printed in Europe, USA, Canada, Australia, Japan

Cover: Foto ©Thomas Meinert / pixelio.de

More available books at **www.hansebooks.com**

LAYS AND LEGENDS

OF

ANCIENT GREECE

BY

JOHN STUART BLACKIE

PROFESSOR OF GREEK IN THE UNIVERSITY OF EDINBURGH

SECOND EDITION

WILLIAM BLACKWOOD AND SONS
EDINBURGH AND LONDON
MDCCCLXXX

JOHN HUNTER, ESQ.

DEAR FRIEND, who by Corstorphine's bosky bower,
From the shrill strife of wrangling law remote,
Reapest the mellow fruits of quiet thought,
Receive in Jeffrey's quaint and ivied tower
This little book.   Though from the grand parade
Of printed verdicts thou hast long been free,
The man who loved the Muse still found in Thee
A judge to value, and a friend to aid.
Thou, the nice student of fine-thoughted Keats,
Mayst find my rhymes cast in too rough a mould
For thy keen sense, fed with essential sweets:
If so, speak free; I'll take thy blame for gold,
And count their coin for brass, with false fair phrase
Who blow the flattering trump before my Lays.

PREFATORY NOTE.

FROM this second edition of the 'Lays and Legends of Ancient Greece' I have excluded all the miscellaneous poems, which occupied about the half of the original edition, but which had no connection with the part which gave the title to the volume. I have also excluded one Hellenic poem — the "Pythagoras"—because its dramatic treatment naturally removed it to my 'Wise Men of Greece,' in which company, accordingly, in an expanded and improved shape, it will be found. The best of the other poems were republished either in my 'Lays of the Highlands and Islands,' or in my 'Songs of Religion and of Life,' in accordance with the category to which they seemed naturally to belong.

J. S. B.

OBAN, 1st October 1880.

CONTENTS.

LAYS AND LEGENDS.

INTRODUCTION.

I.

MUSE of old Hellas, wake again !
   Thou wert not born to die—
And mingle sweet the Classic strain
   With Gothic minstrelsy !
I feel a tingling in my veins,
   My heart is beating strong ;
Let novel-writers count their gains,
   I'll pipe my Doric song.
The wood has warblers great and small ;
God scatters free ; let carpers cavil !

A

There's room in Helicon for all
   That swell the tuneful revel.
On flaming chariot Shelley soars
   Through starry realms serene ;
His volleyed thunder Byron pours
   With lurid flash between ;
Lone in far mountains Wordsworth strolls
   And hums a thoughtful lay,
As a deep river slowly rolls
   Through beds of fruitful clay.
Like a fair country stretching wide
With woods on woods in leafy pride
   And fields of golden grain,
And moors with purple heather glowing,
And healthful breezes bravely blowing,
   Spreads Scott his vast domain.
Not I with these may dare to vie ;
   Nor with thy learnèd lay,
Kehama's bard ! nor prophesy,
   With deep oracular bay,
Like him who sate on Highgate hill
   And taught, with mystic care,

The suckling priests who owned his skill
  To syllogise their prayer.
Far from such eagle-flight be mine!
But while I feel the thrill divine,
  I will not clip my wing;
The beetle, 'neath his horny case,
Hath gauzy pinions that with grace
  Uplift the creeping thing.
Though sober friends forbid the verse,
My old Greek rhyme I will rehearse,
  Like a lone wandering bee
On a hillside, that sips sweet dew
From fragrant blooms of purple hue,
  And drones low minstrelsy.
The modest lay be slow to blame,
Piped more for pleasure than for fame:
Music to harmless souls belongs,
Cold worldly hearts are scant of songs.

II.

The old Greek men, the old Greek men,
   No blinking fools were they;
But with a free and broad-eyed ken
   Looked forth on glorious day.
They looked on the Sun in their cloudless sky,
   And they saw that his light was fair;
And they said that the round full-beaming eye
   Of a blazing god was there.
They looked on the vast spread Earth, and saw
The various-fashioned forms with awe
   Of green and creeping life,
And said—"In every moving form
With buoyant breath and pulses warm,
In flowery crowns, and veinèd leaves,
A goddess dwells, whose bosom heaves
   With organising strife."
They looked and saw the billowy ocean,
With its boundless swell of sleepless motion,
Belting the firm earth, far and wide,
With the flow of its deep untainted tide:

And wondering viewed in its clear blue
    flood
A quick and scaly-glancing brood,
Sporting innumerous in the deep,
With dart, and plunge, and airy leap;
And said—"Full sure a god doth reign
King of this watery wide domain,
And rides in a car of cerulean hue
O'er bounding billows of green and blue;
And in one hand a three-pronged spear
He holds, the sceptre of his fear,
And with the other shakes the reins
Of his steeds, with foamy flowing manes,
    And courses o'er the brine;
And when he lifts his trident mace,
Broad Ocean crisps his placid face,
    And mutters wrath divine;
The big waves rush with hissing crest,
And beat the shore with ample breast,
    And shake the toppling cliff;
A wrathful god hath roused the wave,
Vain is all pilot's skill to save,

And lo ! a deep black-throated grave
   Engulfs the reeling skiff.
Anon, the flood less fiercely flows,
The rifted cloud blue ether shows,
   The windy buffets cease;
Poseidon chafes his heart no more,
His voice constrains the billowy roar.
   And men may sail in peace."
Thus every power that zones the sphere
With forms of beauty and of fear,
In starry sky, on grassy ground,
And in the fishful brine profound,
Were to the hoar Pelasgic men
That peopled erst each Grecian glen,
Gods, or the functions of a god.
Gods were in every sight and sound,
And every spot was hallowed ground
Where these far - wandering patriarchs
     trod.
In the old oak a Dryad dwelt,
The fingers of a nymph were felt
   In the fine-rippled flood;

At drowsy noon, when all is still,

Faunus lay sleeping on the hill,

And strange and bright-eyed gamesome creatures

With hairy limbs and goat-like features,

  Peered from the prickly wood.

Nor less within that mystic realm

Where passions swell and thoughts o'erwhelm,

  Strong ruling powers divine

Were worshipped.   All-controlling Jove

With clear-discerning eye did prove

Each human heart.   The thoughts that move

To pity of the houseless poor,

The kindly hand that opes the door

Of refuge to a wandering wight,

Storm-battered on a starless night,

  Obeyed his law benign.

And when unreined wild passion flew,

And evil hate sharp daggers drew,

  And deathful blows were given,

Dream not that he who fled from man

Escaped the sleepless eyes that scan

  All sinful deeds in Heaven.

Far from the fell avenger's tread
The pale guilt-haunted murderer fled;
O'er many a blasted heath he sped,
The dewy sky his curtain made,
    No sleep might reach his eyes;
For, when he fain would rest, a crew
Of murky-mantled maids from Hell,
Snuffing his blood, his track pursue
And pierce his ears with baleful yell,
    That blissful slumber flies:
Haggard he lives a little space,
    No fatness rounds his eyes;
The Furies' mark is on his face;
Grim leaders of the airy chase
Perplex his path from place to place,
Till stumbling with a blinded fall,
With never a god to hear his call,
    The wasted outcast dies.

III.

Old fables these and fancies old !
   But not, with hasty pride,
Let Logic cold and Reason bold
   Cast these old dreams aside.
Dreams are not false in all their scope ;
   Oft from the sleepy lair
Start giant-shapes of fear and hope
   That, aptly read, declare
Our deepest nature.   God in dreams
   Hath spoken to the wise ;
And in a people's mythic themes
   A people's wisdom lies.
O'er the brown moor some love to roam,
   And with the hammer's dint
To strike from its old chalky home
   The curious-rounded flint ;
Or they with brightening eye will bring,
   From bed of dingy clay,
Some bony frame of a scaly thing
   Unused to garish day,

Lizard or crocodile or snake,
    Or mingled of the three;
Creatures of huge unwieldy make
    That in the primal sea
Paddled, or through the marsh did stalk
    With round and staring eyes,
Before the Serpent learned to talk
    With Eve in Paradise.

Others there be that love to soar
    Sublime in starry realms,
'Mid seas of worlds without a shore,
    Where vasty space o'erwhelms
Man's shrinking soul.   From star to star
    With glass in hand at leisure
They wander, and can tell how far
    The blue highway doth measure
From Earth to Phœbus, and from him
    To the star that wears a belt,
And to our system's extreme rim
    Where never a ray was felt
Of throbbing heat.   These men can write
    The Moon's authentic history,

And of its mass, here dark, there bright,
    Expound the spotted mystery;
How like an apple by the fire
    It swells and cracks, and bubbles,
That no live creature can aspire
    'Mid its volcanic troubles
To breathe; it hath no atmosphere
    For men or salamanders,
But with obedient pale career
    Through old grey Space it wanders
To lamp our Earth. I cannot say
    If this be true or no;
But in a far-diverging way
    My best-loved fancies go.
Man is my theme; Earth is my sphere!
    The struggling fates pursuing
Of earth-born men, I would not hear
    What Sun and Moon are doing.
Give me a tale of human passion,
Of oldest or of newest fashion,
Hard facts, or fictions that contain
Deep-pondered truth's clear-running well,

Like mysteries hid from ken profane
In evangelic parable;
Hoariest oracles that linger
Round Parnassus' rifted hollow,
Where the pale tripod-seated singer
Raved out thy mystic will, Apollo;
Ballad or song, or plaintive ditty
Chanted through the drizzly night,
Amid the hum of peopled city,
By some maimed and woe-worn wight.
Tell me how erst the Lydian king,
    Whom Pelops called his father,
Was borne sublime on eagle's wing
    Where gods immortal gather
To eat ambrosia, and to quaff
    The nectared cup at leisure:
There sate the king at jovial board,
With Heaven's dark-locked high-thundering
        lord,
And shared Olympian jest and laugh,
And blew dull care away like chaff,
    And sipped the deathless pleasure.

O Tantalus! thou wert a man
More blessed than all, since Earth began
   Its weary round to travel;
But placed in Paradise, like Eve,
Thine own damnation thou didst weave
   Without help from the Devil.
Alas! I fear thy tale to tell,
Thou'rt in the deepest pool of Hell,
   And shalt be there for ever.
For why?—When thou on lofty seat
Didst sit, and eat immortal meat
   With Jove, the bounteous Giver,
The gods before thee loosed their tongue,
And many a mirthful ballad sung,
And all their secrets open flung
   Into thy mortal ear.
And thou didst know what no man knows,
How gossip in Olympus goes,
When radiant glasses circle round,
And tinkling Muses beat the ground,
And gods to music's thrilling sound
   Relax their brows severe.

Then Hermes spins his finest fibs,

And grinning Momus splits his ribs,

And Phœbus bright recounts his loves

On grassy slopes, in laurel-groves.

Thou saw'st, when awful Jove unbent

   O'er cups of sparkling sheen,

And on the rounded shoulder leant

   Of Juno, white-armed queen;

But she, with jealous reprobation,

Rated his partial conversation

   With Thetis, not unseen;

Which, when he heard, the Olympian Sire

Gathered his brows in anger dire,

And straight was hushed the festive lyre;

No sound of joyaunce shook the hall,

Dumb fear sate on the lips of all,

And the sweet nectar turned to gall.

And thou didst see how every god

Quailed at the wrathful father's nod;

   But sooty Vulcan then,

With cup in hand and napkin white,

   Tired like a waiting knave,

On that divine assembly bright
   Such rare attendance gave,
And limped with such quaint grace, that
     they
With peals of unextinguished laughter
Shook the wide welkin's beamy rafter;
Nor frowned again, while all were gay,
   The king of gods and men.
All this, and of the heavenly place
   More secrets rare were known
Of mortal men, by Jove's high grace,
   To Tantalus alone.
But witless he such grace to prize;
   And with licentious babble,
He blazed the secrets of the skies
   Through all the human rabble,
And fed the greed of tattlers vain
   With high celestial scandal,
And lent to every itching brain
   And wanton tongue a handle
Against the gods. For which great sin,
   By righteous Jove's command,

In Hell's black pool, up to the chin,
  The thirsty king doth stand:
With parchèd throat, he longs to drink,
  But, when he bends to sip,
The envious waves receding sink,
  And cheat his pining lip.
Such tales delight me roaming free,
  At dusky eve o'er heathy common;
And such I've rhymed—a few—for thee,
  Of kindred fancy, man or woman.
There's labour in a learnèd life
And many a tome with dulness rife
  The patient scholar reads;
He scrapes the ground, and breaks the crust,
And from deep heaps of choking dust
  Redeems the buried seeds;
But here I've cropped the bloom for thee:
Accept these old Greek flowers, free
  From thorns and hateful weeds.

PANDORA.

’Ονόμηνε δε τήνδε γυναῖκα.

Πανδώρην, ὅτι πάντες Ολύμπια δώματ’ ἔχοντες

δῶρον ἐδώρησαν, πῆμ’ ἀνδράσιν ἀλφηστῇσιν.—HESIOD.

I.

PROMETHEUS was a famous moulder
  In the old Greek time,
Ere the blind Smyrnéan minstrel [1]
  Wove his pictured rhyme.
Sprung from oldest Earth and Heaven's
  . Titan progeny,
Hardy-limbed, and sturdy labour's
  Primal type was he.

One day, 'neath the slanting chariot
   Of the cooler sun,
He did sweat, his task to finish
   Ere the day was done.
With the finely plastic finger's
   Soft-subduing sway,
He did shape the breathing feature
   From the senseless clay,
Like a god : and therefore jealous
   Of such godlike skill,
Mighty Jove the purpose nursed
   To break his hardy will.
Vainly ; for Jove's fire the Titan
   In a smoking reed,
From the glowing empyrean
   Drew with furtive speed ;
And by might of all subduing
   Chymick fire had taught
Arts to crudest-witted mortals
   From wild wanderings brought.
Him and them the harsh Olympian,
   From his throne sublime,

Feared, lest they with strong invention
   To the stars should climb
And mar his new dominion.   Wherefore
   He to daze the sight
Of the Titan wise prepares,
   With sensuous splendour bright.
With Apollo's slanting chariot,
   And the cooler ray,
He hath sent his minion Hermes,
   Winged with speed to-day,
Shod with guile to where the Titan
   Kneads the pliant clay.
Lo! he comes, the nimble-sandalled
   Airy-footed god,
And with softly-soothing motion
   Waves his golden rod.
Nor comes alone: behind him breathing
   Rosy beauty warm,
Veiled with glory iridescent,
   Floats a gentle form.
Oh, she is fair beyond compare!
   Her the thunderer high

With all beauty's bravery pranked
    To trick the Titan's eye.
Her thy forging wit, Hephæstus,
    Cunningly did frame ;
Every god his virtue gave
    To make a perfect dame.
With soft-swelling smoothness Venus
    Rounded every limb,
And her full deep eye cerulean
    Dashed with wanton whim.
Round her chiselled mouth the Graces
    Wove their wreathings rare,
All his sunny radiance Phœbus
    Showered upon her hair.
Juno gave the lofty stature
    That beseems the queen,
Dian the light-footed grace
    That trips the springy green.
Tuned her throat the grace of Muses
    To the perfect bird ;
Hermes from her tongue sweet-suasive
    Winged the witching word.

With a various-pictured vesture,
    Woven thin and fine,
From subtle-threaded loom Athena
    Clad the shape divine.
Thus with gifts well-dowered, Pandora,
    Now by Hermes led,
With a sudden beauty glorious,
    Floods the sober shed
Where the patient Titan labours;
    Him in wonder lost
Thus with glib address Jove's courier
    Smartly doth accost:
" Son of Themis, lofty-counselled,
    This from Hermes know,
Jove the patient cunning honouring
    Of his whilom foe,
Sends for solace of thy labour,
    And thy thanks to claim,
Gift of gods this glory-garnished
    Beauty-breathing dame.
Shake the dust from off thy vesture;
    Pleasure after pain,

The just meed that virtue merits,
    Clears the cloudy brain."
Thus the god; but wise Prometheus
    Turns his face away,
And with cool design deep-thoughted
    Kneads the yielding clay:
Nay, quoth Hermes, surely madness
    Makes the wise her own,
Or he to stony labour used
    Himself is grown a stone!
Charm his ear attendant Muses,
    With quick rapture thrill
Every life-string! mighty Music
    Tames the stoutest will.
Spake the god; and like bright wavelets
    Of the sounding sea
Filled the Titan's ear a gentle
    Rush of melody;
Sounds as when the quire of Phœbus
    Trip with tinkling feet
Round thy fair fount, Aganippe,
    Singing clear and sweet;

Sounds as when goat-footed Faunus
 In a mossy nook
Pipes his drowsy reed at noon-day
 To the murmuring brook;
Sounds so rare as Jove Olympian
 Drinks with ravished ears
When he hears the beat canorous
 Of the travelling spheres;
Every sound that voiceful April
 Lends the floating breeze,
Laden with the fragrant burden
 From the fresh-tipt trees:
With such sweet assailing voices
 Cunning Hermes plied
Wise Prometheus; but the Titan
 The strong spell defied.
Eye and ear from soft seducement
 Stern he turned away,
Till his faithful hand had ended
 With its task the day.

II.

On a grassy slope recumbent,
    Epimetheus lies;
Epimetheus, witless brother
    Of Prometheus wise.
In the pleasant sun he basketh,
    And with dreamful eyes,
Weeting half, and half unweeting,
    Follows, as it flies,
Every shade that sweeps the meadow;
    And with cradled ear,
The mingled hum of summer voices
    Drowsily doth hear.
Thus at ease supine he lieth,
    Nursing fancies vain,
Every frothy thought that bubbles
    From an idle brain,
Every wish that fond belief
    May shape into a creed,
Every floating loose ideal
    That begets no deed,

Thoughts of light and cloudy tissue,
    Thoughts of sunbeams wove,
Thoughts of rapture more than earthly,
    Thoughts of rosy love.
Him thus in luxurious musing
    Cunning Hermes found,
From his airy pathway lighting
    With a nimble bound,
And with him the fair Pandora;
    By the wise rejected,
On the witless now she beams
    With beauty unexpected,
And veiled in rosy splendour glorious.
    Epimetheus gazes
On the fair with blank emotion;
    While with smooth-trimmed phrases,
Thus the courier speaks—" Brave Titan,
    This from Hermes know,
Jove, whom thy proud brother vainly
    Deems the Titan's foe,
Sends me here on blissful mission,
    Gracious to impart

Fruitage to the fairest dreams
    That stir thy lofty heart.
Earth-born thou, but not for earthy
    Plodding wert thou born,
With axe and spade to drudge inglorious
    From the mist-wreathed morn
To the grey-veiled eve; thy spirit's
    Climate is the sky;
Traitor to himself who feareth
    Where it points to fly.
Flesh and blood with bread he feedeth,
    But immortal Jove
Feeds the soul that pants for beauty
    With immortal love.
Lo! thy heart's divinely-thirsting
    Fever to abate,
He hath sent this glory-garnished,
    Beauty-breathing mate."
Mute the spell-struck Epimetheus
    Eyed the wonder rare,
Heedless of what wiles Kronion
    Screened beneath the fair.

And in tranceful adoration
    Kissed his knees the ground ;
While from rapture-glowing breast
    He poured the vow profound —
" Bless thee, bless thee, gentle Hermes !
    Once I sinned and strove
Vainly, with my haughty brother,
    'Gainst Olympian Jove.
Now my doubts his love hath vanquished ;
    Evil knows not he
Whose free-streaming grace prepared
    Such gift of gods for me.
Henceforth I and fair Pandora,
    Joined in holy love,
Only one in Heaven will worship,
    Cloud-compelling Jove."
Thus he ; and from the god received
    The glorious gift of Jove,
And with fond embracement clasped her,
    Thrilled by potent love ;
And in loving dalliance with her
    Lived from day to day,

While her bounteous smiles diffusive
  Scared dull care away.
By the mountain, by the river,
  'Neath the shaggy pine,
By the cool and mossy fountain
  Where clear waters shine,
He with her did lightly stray
  Or softly did recline,
Drinking sweet intoxication
  From that form divine.
One day when the moon had wheeled
  Four honeyed weeks away,
From her chamber came Pandora
  Decked with trappings gay,
And before fond Epimetheus
  Fondly she did stand,
A box all bright with lucid opal
  In her smooth white hand.
Dainty box! cried Epimetheus,
  Dainty well may't be,
Quoth Pandora,—curious Vulcan
  Framed it cunningly;

Jove bestowed it in my dowry :
  Like bright Phœbus' ray,
It shines without ; within what wealth
  I know not to this day.
Let me see, quoth Epimetheus,
  What my touch can do !
And swiftly to his finger's call
  The box wide open flew ;
O Heaven ! O Hell ! what Pandemonium
  In the pouncet dwells !
How it quakes, and how it quivers !
  How it seethes and swells !
Steams in snaky twine upwreathing,
  Wave on wave is spread !
Like a charnel-vault 'tis breathing
  Vapours of the dead !
Fumes on fumes as from a throat
  Of sooty Vulcan rise,
Clouds of red and blue and yellow
  Blotting out the skies.
And the air with noisome stenches,
  As from things that rot,

Chokes the breather,—exhalations
   From the infernal pot.
And amid the writhing vapours
   Ghastly shapes I see
Of dire diseases, Epimetheus,
   Launched on Earth by thee;
A loathsome crew! some lean and dwindled,
   Some with boils and blains
Blistered, some with tumours swollen,
   And water in the veins.
Some with purple blotches bloated,
   Some with humours flowing
Putrid, some with creeping tetter
   Like a lichen growing
O'er the dry skin scaly-crusted;
   Some with twisted spine
Dwarfing low with torture slow
   The human form divine:
Limping some, some limbless lying;
   Fever with frantic air,
And pale consumption veiling death
   With looks serenely fair.

All the troop of cureless evils
　　Rushing reinless forth
From thy damned box, Pandora,
　　Seize the tainted Earth;
And to lay the marshalled legions
　　Of our fiendish pains,
Hope alone, a sorry charmer,
　　In the box remains.
Epimetheus knew the dolours,
　　But he knew too late;
Jealous Jove himself now vainly
　　Would revoke the Fate.
And he cursed the fair Pandora,
　　But he cursed in vain;
Still to fools the fleeting pleasure
　　Buys the lasting pain.

PROMETHEUS.[2]

Πᾶσας τέχνας βροτοῖσιν ἐκ Προμηθέως.—ÆSCHYLUS.

I.

Blow blustering winds; loud thunders roll!
Swift lightnings rend the fervid pole
With frequent flash! his hurtling hail
Let Jove down-fling! hoarse Neptune flail
The stubborn rock, and give free reins
To his dark steeds with foamy manes
That paw the strand!—such wrathful fray
Touches not me, who, even as they,
Immortal tread this lowly sod,
    Born of the gods a god.

II.

Jove rules above; Fate willed it so.
'Tis well; Prometheus rules below.
Their gusty game let wild winds play,
And clouds on clouds in thick array
Muster dark armies in the sky;
Be mine a harsher trade to ply,
This solid Earth, this rocky frame
To mould, to conquer, and to tame;
And to achieve the toilsome plan,
My workman shall be MAN.

III.

The Earth is young.   Even with these eyes
I saw the molten mountains rise
From out the seething deep, while Earth
Shook at the portent of their birth.
I saw from out the primal mud
The reptiles crawl of dull cold blood,

C

While wingèd lizards with broad stare
Peered through the raw and misty air.
Where then was Cretan Jove? where then
    This king of gods and men?

IV.

When naked from his mother Earth,
Weak and defenceless, man crept forth,
And on mis-tempered solitude
Of unploughed field and unclipt wood
Gazed rudely; when with brutes he fed
On acorns, and his stony bed
In dark unwholesome caverns found;
No skill was then to till the ground,
No help came then from him above,
    This tyrannous-blustering Jove.

V.

The Earth is young. Her latest birth,
This weakling man, my craft shall girth

With cunning strength.   Him I will take,
And in stern arts my scholar make.
This smoking reed, in which I hold
The empyrean spark, shall mould
Rock and hard steel to use of man ;
He shall be as a god to plan
And forge all things to his desire
　　By alchemy of fire.

VI.

These jagged cliffs that flout the air,
Harsh granite blocks so rudely bare,
Wise Vulcan's art and mine shall own,
To piles of shapeliest beauty grown.
The steam that snorts vain strength away
Shall serve the workman's curious sway
Like a wise child ; as clouds that sail
White winged before the summer gale,
The smoking chariot o'er the land
　　Shall roll, at his command.

VII.

Blow, winds, and crack your cheeks ! my home
Stands firm beneath Jove's thundering dome,
This stable Earth.   Here let me work !
The busy spirits, that eager lurk
Within a thousand labouring breasts,
Here let me rouse ; and whoso rests
From labour let him rest from life.
To live 's to strive ; and in the strife
To move the rock, and stir the clod,
　　Man makes himself a god.

THE NAMING OF ATHENS.[3]

Παρθένοι ὀμβροφόροι
ἔλθωμεν λιπαράν χθόνα Πάλλαδος, εὔανδρον γᾶν
Κέκροπος ὀψόμεναι πολυήρατον.—ARISTOPHANES.

On the rock of Erectheus the ancient, the hoary,
    That rises sublime from the far-stretching plain,
Sate Cecrops, the first in Athenian story
    Who guided the fierce by the peace-loving rein.
Eastward away by the flowery Hymettus,
    Westward where Salamis gleams in the bay,
Northward, beneath the high-peaked Lycabettus,
    He numbered the towns that rejoiced in his sway.
Pleased was his eye with the muster, but rested
    At length where he sate with an anxious love,

When he thought on the strife of the mighty
    broad-breasted
  Poseidon, with Pallas, the daughter of Jove;
For the god of the earth-shaking ocean had sworn it,
  The city of Cecrops should own him supreme,
Or the land and the people should ruefully mourn
    it,
  Swamped by the swell of the broad ocean-stream.
Lo! from the North, as he doubtfully ponders,
  A light shoots far-streaming; the welkin it fills;
Southward from Parnes bright-bearded it wanders,
  Swift as the courier-fires from the hills.
Far on the flood of the winding Cephissus,
  There gleams like the shape of a serpentine rod,
Shimmers the tide of the gentle Ilissus
  With radiance from Hermes the messenger-god.
'Twas he: on the Earth with light touch he de-
    scended,
  And struck the grey rock with his gold-gleaming
    rod,
While Cecrops with low-hushed devotion attended,
  And reverent awe to the voice of the god.

" Noble autochthon ! a message I bear thee,

   From Jove in Olympus who regally sways ;

Wise is the god the dark trouble to spare thee,—

   Blest is the heart that believes and obeys.

On the peaks of Olympus, the bright snowy-

      crested,

   The gods are assembled in council to-day ;

The wrath of Poseidon, the mighty broad-breasted,

   'Gainst Pallas, the spear-shaking maid, to allay ;

And thus they decree—that Poseidon offended,

   And Pallas shall bring forth a gift to the place ;

On the hill of Erectheus the strife shall be ended,

   When she with her spear, and the god with his

      mace,

Shall strike the quick rock ; and the gods shall

      deliver

   The sentence as Justice shall order ; and thou

Shalt see thy loved city established for ever

   With Jove for a judge, and the Styx for a vow."

He spake ; and, while Cecrops devoutly was

      bending,

   To worship the knees of the herald of Jove,

Shone from the pole, in full glory descending,
  The cloud-car that bore the bright gods from
    above,
Beautiful, glowing with many-hued splendour.
  O what a kinship of godhead was there!
Juno the stately, full-eyed; and the tender
  Bland-beaming Venus, so rosily fair;
Dian the huntress, with arrow and quiver,
  And airily tripping with light-footed grace;
Apollo, with radiance poured like a river
  Diffusive o'er Earth, from his joy-giving face;
Bacchus the rubicund; and with fair tresses,
  The bright-fruited Ceres, and Vesta the chaste;
And the god that delights in fair Venus' caresses,
  Stout Mars, in his mail adamantine encased.
Then, while wild thunders innocuous gather
  Round his brow, diademed green with the
    oak,
On the rock of Erectheus descended the Father,
  And thus to good Cecrops serenely he spoke:
" Kingly autochthon! the sorrow deep-rooted
  That gnaweth thy heart, the Olympians know;

Too long with Poseidon hath Pallas disputed,—
   This day shall be peace, or great Jove is their
     foe."
He spake; and a sound like the rushing of ocean,
   From smooth-grained Pentelicus, seizes their
     ears;
From his home in Eubœa, with haughty commotion,
   To the place of the judgment, the sea-monarch
     nears.
On the waves of the wind his blue car travelled
     proudly,
   Proudly his locks to the breeze floated free,
Snorted his mane-tossing coursers, and loudly
   Blew from the tortuous conch of the sea
Shrill Tritons the clear-throated blast undisputed,
   That curleth the wild wave, and cresteth the main;
While Nereids around him, the fleet foamy-footed,
   Floated, as floated his undulant rein.
Thus on the rock of Erectheus alighted
   The god of the sea, and the rock with his mace
Smote; for he knew that the gods were invited
   To judge of the gift that he gave to the place.

Lo! at the touch of his trident a wonder!

    Virtue to Earth from his deity flows:

From the rift of the flinty rock cloven asunder,

    A dark-watered fountain ebullient rose.

Inly elastic with airiest lightness

    It leapt, till it cheated the eyesight; and, lo!

It showed in the sun, with a various brightness,

    The fine-woven hues of the rain-loving bow.

" WATER IS BEST!" cried the mighty broad-breasted

    Poseidon; "O Cecrops, I offer to thee

To ride on the back of the steeds foamy-crested,

    That toss their wild manes on the huge-heaving

        sea.

The globe thou shalt mete on the path of the waters,

    To thy ships shall the ports of far ocean be free;

The isles of the sea shall be counted thy daughters,

    The pearls of the East shall be treasured for

        thee!"

He spake; and the gods, with a high-sounding

    pæan,

    Applauded; but Jove hushèd the many-voiced

        tide;

" For now, with the lord of the briny Ægean,

    Athena shall strive for the city," he cried.

" See, where she comes!"—and she came, like

    Apollo,

    Serene with the beauty ripe wisdom confers;

The clear-scanning eye, and the sure hand to follow

    The mark of the far-sighted purpose, was hers.

Strong in the mail of her father she standeth,

    And firmly she holds the strong spear in her

    hand ;

But the wild hounds of war with calm power she

    commandeth,

    And fights but to pledge surer peace to the land.

Chastely the blue-eyed approached, and, surveying

    The council of wise-judging gods without fear,

The nod of her lofty-throned father obeying,

    She struck the grey rock with her nice-tempered

    spear.

Lo ! from the touch of the virgin a wonder !

    Virtue to Earth from her deity flows :

From the rift of the flinty rock cloven asunder,

    An olive-tree greenly luxuriant rose—

Green, but yet pale, like an eye-drooping maiden,
 Gentle, from full-blooded lustihood far;
No broad-staring hues for rude pride to parade
 in,
 No crimson to blazon the banners of war.
Mutely the gods, with a calm consultation,
 Pondered the fountain, and pondered the tree;
And the heart of Poseidon, with high expectation,
 Throbbed, till great Jove thus pronounced the
 decree:
" Son of my father, thou mighty broad-breasted
 Poseidon, the doom that I utter is true;
Great is the might of thy waves foamy-crested,
 When they beat the white halls of the screaming
 sea-mew:
Great is the pride of the keel when it danceth,
 Laden with wealth, o'er the light-heaving wave;
When the East to the West, gaily floated, advanceth,
 With a word from the wise, and a help from the
 brave.
But Earth, solid Earth, is the home of the mortal,
 That toileth to live, and that liveth to toil;

And the green olive-tree twines the wreath of his
    portal,
  Who peacefully wins his sure bread from the
    soil."
Thus Jove; and aloft the great council celestial
  Rose, and the sea-god rolled back to the sea;
But Athena gave Athens her name, and terrestrial
  Joy, from the oil of the green olive-tree.

BELLEROPHON.[1]

"Ος τᾶς ὀφίωδεος υἱόν ποτε Γόργονος
ἦ πολλ' ἀμφὶ κρουνοῖς
Πάγασον ζεῦξαι ποθέων ἔπαθεν
Πρίν γέ οἱ χρυσάμπυκα κούρα χαλινὸν
Παλλὰς ἤνεγκε.—PINDAR.

'Αλλ' ὅτε δὴ καὶ κεῖνος ἀπήχθετο πᾶσι θεοῖσιν
ἤτοι ὁ κὰπ πεδίον τὸ 'Αλήιον οἶος ἀλᾶτο
ὃν θυμὸν κατέδων πάτον ἀνθρώπων ἀλεείνων.
—HOMER.

I.

The sun shines bright on Ephyré's height,
And right and left, with billowy might,
    Poseidon rules the sea ;

But not the Sun that rules above,

Nor strong Poseidon, nor great Jove,

Can look with looks of favouring love,

  Bellerophon, on thee.

There's blood upon thy hands ; the hounds

  Of hell pursue thy path ;

Nor they within rich Corinth's bounds

  Shall slack their vengeful wrath.

Black broods the sky above thy head,

The Earth breeds serpents at thy tread,

  The Furies' foot hath found thee ;

A baleful pest their presence brings,

A curse to peasants and to kings ;

The horrid shadow of their wings

  Turns day to darkness round thee.

Flee o'er the Argive hills, and there,

With suppliant branch and pious prayer,

  Thou shalt not crave in vain

Some prince, whose hands not worthless hold

The sceptre of Phoroneus old,

To cleanse thy guilt, and make thee bold

  To look on men again.

II.

Darkly the Nemean forests frown,
  Where Apesantian Jove
From his broad altar-seat looks down
  On the Ogygian grove.
Fierce roars the lion from his den
In Tretus' long and narrow glen;
  And many a lawless man
Here by the stony water-bed
Lists the lone traveller's errant tread,
  And wakes the plundering clan.
Here be thy flight, Bellerophon,
  But danger fear thou none;
For she, the warlike and the wise,
Jove's blue-eyed daughter, from surprise
  Secure shall lead thee on.
He flees: and, where the priestess bears
  To Hera on the hill
The sacred keys, he pours his prayers,
  And drinks the scanty rill.

He flees : and now before his eye,
With wall and gate and bulwark high,
And many a tower that fronts the sky,
        And many a covered way,
Strong Tiryns stands, whose massy blocks
Were torn by Cyclops from the rocks,
        And piled in vast array.
Here Prœtus reigns; and here, at length,
The suppliant flings his jaded strength
        Before a friendly door;
And now from hot pursuit secure,
And from blood-guiltiness made pure,
        His heart shall fear no more.

III.

The princely Prœtus opes his gate,
And on the fugitive's dark fate
        Smiles gracious; him from fear,
And terror of the scourge divine,
He purifies with blood of swine
        And sprinkled water clear.

D

O blessed was the calm that now
Lulled his racked brain, and smoothed his
      brow !
    Nor wildly now did roll
His sleepless eyes; from gracious Jove
Came down the gentle dew of love,
    And soothed his wounded soul.
And grateful was the face of man
To heart now free from Furies' ban,
    And sweet the festive lyre.
Fair was each sight on that fair day,
Spread forth in beautiful array,
    To move the heart's desire.
Each manly sport and social game
Thrilled with new joy his re - strung
      frame,
    And waked the living fire.
Antéa saw him poise the dart,
In the fleet race the foremost start,
And lawless Venus smote her heart ;
    She loved her lord no more :

As no chaste woman sues she sued,
Her guest the partial hostess wooed,
 And lavished beauty's store
Of luminous smiles and glistening tears,
And silvery speech; but he reveres
The rights of hospitable Jove,
Chastely repels her perilous love,
 Nor hears her parley more.

IV.

Who slights a woman's love cuts deep,
And wakes a brood of snakes that sleep
 Beneath a bed of roses.
The lustful wife of Prœtus now
To earthly Venus vows a vow,
 And in her heart proposes
A fiendish thing. She, with the pin
That bound her peplos, pierced the skin
 Of her smooth-rounded arm;

And when the crimson stream began
To trickle down, she instant ran,
    And with a feigned alarm
Roused all her maids, and in the ear
Of the fond Prœtus, quick to hear,
    She poured the piteous lie,
That the false guest had sought to move
Her loyal-mated heart with love,
And with rude hands had dared assail
Her virtue, cased in surer mail
    Than Dian's panoply:
Then, more to stir his wrathful mood,
She bared her arm that streamed with blood,
    And scared his jealous eye.
Hot boiled his Argive heart; his eyes
Flash vengeance; but himself denies
    The reins to his own spleen.
His public face in smiles is dressed,
He joins the banquet with the rest,
And tells the tale, and plies the jest,
    With easy social mien;

And to his high Corinthian guest
    Lets not a thought be seen.
" Take here," quoth he, " thou high-souled knight,
To Iobates the Lycian wight,
    The brother of my queen,
These tablets; he will honour thee
Even more than I ; and thou shalt see
A famous and a fruitful land,
With all Apollo's beauty bland,
    And leafy splendour green."
Uprose the knight with willing feet,
His heart was light, his pace was fleet ;
Girt for the road and venture bold,
He left the strong Tirynthian hold,
    And gaily wends his way
O'er steep Arachne's ridge, till he
Passed Æsculapius' sacred fane,
Whose virtue soothes each racking pain,
And reached, with foot untired, the sea
That beats with billows bounding free
    The Epidaurian bay.

V.

Thoughtful a moment here he stood,
And watched the never-sleeping flood,
    The ever-changing wave :
He knew no danger, feared no foes,
But from his heart a prayer uprose
    To her that guards the brave.
Wise prayer; for scarce the words are
        gone
From thy free mouth, Bellerophon,
    When, smote with holy awe,
Even at thy side, in light arrayed,
Serene with placid power displayed,
The chaste strong-fathered blue-eyed maid
    Thy wondering vision saw ;
And in her hand—O wondrous sight !—
    A wingèd steed she led,
That bent the knee before the knight,
    And bowed its lofty head.
" Fear not, thou son of Æolus' race,—
    Dear to the gods art thou ;

This steed, by strong Poseidon's mace
That leapt to life, through airy space
    Shall safely waft thee now."
Thus spake the goddess, wise as fair;
And with the word, dissolved in air,
    Was seen no more. The knight
Brushed from his eyes the dazzling
        glare,
    And scarce believed his sight.
But, when he saw the steed was there,
He winged to Heaven a hasty prayer,
    And for the airy flight
Buckled his purpose. Mounted now
    With rapid wheel he soars,
O'er creek and crag, and rocky brow,
    And swift-receding shores.
A lovely sight was there, I trow,
    Where high on wingèd oars
He clove the blue. The broad sea's
        face
With multitudinous-dimpled grace,
    Immense before him lay,

With many a coast far - stretching
seen,
And many a high-cliffed isle between,
And many a winding bay.
High o'er Œnone's isle he sails,
Where Æacus' justest law prevails,
And masted armies ride;
O'er rocky Sunium's pillar'd steep,
Where Pallas guards the Attic deep,
He swept with airy pride.
Seriphus, Ceos, Syros, saw
His meteor-steed with wondering awe;
And sacred Delos deemed
Apollo's self was travelling o'er
The empyrean's fervid floor,
That with such brightness gleamed.
Swift o'er the Bacchic isle he glides,
Where music mingles with the tides
From many a Mænad throat.
And nigh to Caria's craggy shore,
Cos with her blushing winy store
His sweeping view may note.

Anon, sublime he soars above
Thy temple, Atabyrian Jove,
    The lord of cloudless Rhodes,
Where Telchins wise, with busy clamour,
Who shape the steel 'neath skilful hammer,
    Possess their famed abodes :
And swiftly then he swoops, I ween,
Down on the steeps of Cragus green,
    Into the pleasant plain,
Where Xanthus rolls his yellow stream,
And Phœbus lights with glorious gleam
    The Patarean plain.
Here he alights.   His heavenly steed,
With instant eye-outstripping speed,
    Scorning the earthly loam,
Wheels eastward far with vans sonorous,
And o'er the rosy peaks of Taurus
    Sails to his starry home.

VI.

The Xanthian gate is wide and free;
 The Xanthian towers are high;
The Xanthian streets are fair to see;
 The knight, with wondering eye,
Beholds, and enters.   To the king
Close-circling throngs the stranger bring,
 And scan him o'er and o'er;
Curious that one so bright and trim,
And with such light unwearied limb,
 Had reached the Lycian shore.
With kindly heart the Xanthian lord
Opes his high hall and spreads his board
 And pours the Coan wine;
Nor question asked (for Jove gives free
To all a questless courtesy)
 Till days were numbered nine.
His tablets then the knight presents;
The monarch scans their dire contents,
 For here 'twas written plainly,

" If thou dost hate who works amiss,
Let not his hand that beareth this

  Have sinned against me vainly;
Thy Prœtus." Sore vexed was the king
That he must do no gracious thing

  Against so brave a guest;
But vows were strong, and family bonds;
Therefore, composed, he thus responds—

  "Brave knight, a fearful pest
Afflicts this land : a monster dire,
With terror armed, and breathing fire,

  In Cragus holds her den,
Chimera named : with savage jaw
She bites, and with voracious maw

  Consumes both beasts and men.
This hideous form its birth did take
From hoar Echidna, virgin-snake,

  Who to that fiery blaster,
Typhon, Cilicia's curse of yore,
This triform goatish portent bore,
With serpent's sting and lion's roar,

  Our Lycian land's disaster.

Harmless at first, for sport 'twas bred
 By Caria's thoughtless king,
And by his innocent children led
 Obedient to a string.
Anon its hellish blood grew hot ;
 It breathed a breath of fire,
And tainted every household spot
 With gouts of poison dire.
Full grown at length, and fierce and bold,
She ranges freely through each fold,
 And licks the fleecy slaughter ;
And, when her humour waxes wild,
No flesh she spares of man or child,
 Echidna's gory daughter.
Now hear me, noble Glaucus' son,
Most valiant knight, Bellerophon ;
Thou hast a face that seems to court
A dangerous business as a sport—
 This thing I ask thee then ;
Wilt thou go forth, and dare to tame
This murtherous monster breathing flame,
And win thyself a deathless name
 Among the Xanthian men ?

VII.

Thus he—(for in his heart he thought
Such venture must with life be bought).
    But brave Bellerophon
Guileless received the guileful plan,
And, as an eager-purposed man,
    Buckled his armour on.
Alone he went : of such emprise
    With this bold-breasted stranger
No one shall share, a herald cries,
    The glory or the danger.
By Xanthus' stream he wends him then,
And leftward up the hollow glen,
Where Pandarus' city, like a tower,
Rises begirt with rocky power ;
    Then upward still he goes,
Where black - browed mountains round him
      lower
And, 'neath chill winter's grisly bower,
    The sunless water flows.

Upon a steep rock hoar with eld
A yawning cave his eye beheld,
High-perched; and to that cave no trace
Of road upon the mountain's face,
    But, like an eagle's nest,
Sublime it hung.   He looked again,
And from the cave a tawny mane
    Shook o'er the rocky crest:
And now a lion's head forth came,
And now, O Heaven! long tongues of
    flame
    Ran wreathing round the hill.
No fear the son of Glaucus knew,
    But pricked his forward will,
The rock-perched monster to pursue:
Now right, now left, he sought a clue
    To thread that steep-faced hill;
Hour after hour no pause he knew,
Till night came down with sable hue,
    And found him searching still.
Hid in the tangled brakes around
Next morn a rugged chasm he found,

That oped into an archway wide,
Right through the hollow mountain-side:
    Here plunged the knight; and then
With fervid foot emerging, speeds
Along a rocky ledge, that leads
    To dire Chimera's den.
The monster hears his quickening tread,
    And with a hideous roar
Trails forth its length, and shows its head
    And mouth that dripped with gore.
The brave knight drew his sword, and flew
    Like lightning on the foe,
And on its hide of horny pride
    Dealt ringing blow on blow.
In vain; that hide, Bellerophon,
Dipt in the flood of Acheron,
    Is proof at every pore;
And where thy steel doth vainly hack,
A goat's head rising on its back
    With living fire streams o'er;
And from behind, a serpent's tail,
    With many mouths that hisses,

Rears round about thee like a flail,
　　To give thee poisoned kisses.
The flame, the smoke, the sulphurous breath
　　Doth choke thy mortal life :
Spare that dear life, for only death
　　Can grow from such a strife.
Backward the flame-scorched hero sped,
And as he went, upon his tread
　　The roaring Terror came.
Along the ridge, so sharp and jaggy,
Huge-limbed it strode, stiff-maned and shaggy,
　　And swathed with sevenfold flame.
Down through the archway opening wide,
Far through the hollow mountain-side,
　　It drove him wrathful on ;
Then through the black jaws of the rock
Down hurled him with a rumbling shock,
　　And heaved a huge sharp stone
Blocking the rift.　There in the vale,
With flickering life, all scorched and pale,
　　Was left Bellerophon.

VIII.

The evening dew was clear and cold :
Upon the harsh ungrateful mould,
All stiff and stark the hero bold
    Lay through the dreamless night ;
But when the face of peering day
Shot o'er the cliff its crimson ray,
With aching frame, as low he lay,
    Sleep seized the weary knight,—
A blissful sleep ; for, when the sense
Was bound with blindness most intense,
    With sharp-eyed soul he saw,
Ev'n at his side, in light arrayed,
Serene with placid power displayed,
The chaste strong - fathered blue - eyed
      maid,
    And worshipped her with awe ;
And in her hand—a well-known sight—
    The wingèd steed she led,

E

That bent the knee before the knight,
　　And meekly bowed its head.
Raptured he woke; with sense now clear
　　He saw the Jove-born maid,
And in her hand a massive spear,
　　Firm-planted, she displayed;
And thus she spoke: "Ephyrian knight,
　　Dear to the gods art thou;
Not vainly did thy prayer invite
My aid, to wing thy airy flight
　　To Cragus' rocky brow.
A friendly god is thy provider;
　　If thou hast wisely planned,
Fear not; the steed doth wait the rider,
　　The spear doth claim the hand.
That snake-born monster's horny hide,
　　That was not made to feel,
May never yield life's crimson tide
　　To sharpest Rhodian steel:
But with this spear from Vulcan's forge,
Right through the mouth in the deep gorge
　　If thou shalt pierce it, then

The dire Chimera breathing flame
Thou with a hero's hand shalt tame,
And win thyself a glorious name
    Among the Xanthian men."
Upstood the knight, with hope elate,
And felt the aching pain abate
    From all his sore-bruised limbs;
The wingèd steed he straight bestrode,
And to Chimera's black abode
    Through liquid air he swims.
The deep-mouthed Terror 'gan to bray,
The forky fire-tongues 'gan to play,
The fretful serpents hissed dismay
    Round all the rocky wall;
But, with direct unwavering speed,
The rider and the heavenly steed
Rushed to achieve the fearless deed,
    At glorious danger's call.
The knight, with searching eye, did note
The centre of the roaring throat,
And, while it gaped with gory jaws
    To thunder fear around,

Forward he rode—nor any pause,

But right into Chimera's gorge

He drove the spear from Vulcan's forge,

    And fixed it in the ground.

Up from the back the fell goat's head

    Rose, rough with tumid ire,

And right and left long tongues were

    spread

    Of forky-flaming fire;

But with immortal strength the steed

    Flaps his huge vans around,

And straight the eager spires recede,

    And harmless lick the ground.

Cowed lie the snakes, and, with quick eye.

A tender place the knight did spy,

    Where the neck joined the back;

There with a fatal swoop he came,

And through the fount of living flame

    He cuts with fierce attack.

Down dropt the goat's head in its gore,

And with a sharp and brazen roar

    The writhing lion dies.

The palsied snakes, with stiffened fang,
Like lifeless leaves unconscious hang;
And, belching rivers of black gore
Upon the clotted rocky floor,
    The smoking carcass lies.

IX.

A famous man was Glaucus' son
    Then when Chimera died;
In Lycian land like him was none
    In glory and in pride.
At public feast beside the king
He sate; him did the minstrel sing
    With various-woven lays;
And old men in the halls were gay,
And maidens smiled, and matrons grey,
And eager boys would cease their play
    To sound the hero's praise.
The Xanthian burghers, wealthy men,
Chose the best acres in the glen
    Beside the fattening river,—

Acres where corn would goodliest grow,
Or vines with richest purple glow;
These, free from burden, they bestow
  On Glaucus' son for ever.
The Xanthian king, to Prœtus bound,
For other dangers looks around,
  And finds, but finds in vain.
'Gainst the stout Solymi to fight
He sent the brave Ephyrian knight,
  With hope he might be slain;
But from the stiff embrace of Mars
He soon returned, and showed his
    scars,
  To glad the Xanthian plain
A Lycian army then he led
Against the maids unhusbanded,
  Where surly Pontus roars.
Before his spear the Amazon yields;
The breastless host, with moonèd
    shields,
Far o'er Thermodon's famous fields
  He drove to Colchian shores.

The Xanthian king despairs the strife—
" Let Prœtus fight for Prœtus' wife ;
Not I will tempt the charmèd life
    Of valiant Glaucus' son ! "
Nor more against the gods he strives,
But with free hand his daughter gives
    To brave Bellerophon.

X.

A prosperous man was Glaucus' son
Then when the queenly maid he won,
    The pride of Lycian land :
The Lycian lords obey his nod,
The people hail him as a god,
    And own his high command.
Fearless he lived without annoy,
Plucking the bloom of every joy ;
    For still, to help his need,
Jove's blue-eyed daughter, when he prayed,
Was present with her heavenly aid,
    And lent the wingèd steed.

His heart with pride was lifted high
Beyond the bounds of earth to fly
Impious he weened, and scale the sky,
    And sit with Jove sublime.
Upward and northward far he sails,
O'er Carian crags and Phrygian vales,
    And blest Mæonia's clime.
The orient breezes round him blowing
He feels; with light the ether glowing;
And from the planets in their spheres
Beating wise march, with charmèd
      ears
    Drinks in the mystic chime.
Bursts far Olympus on his view
Snowy, with gleams of rosy hue;
    And round the heavenly halls,
All radiant with immortal blue
The golden battlements he knew,
    And adamantine walls.
And on the walls, with dizzy awe,
Full many a shapely form he saw
    Of stately grace divine:

The furious Mars with terror crested,
Poseidon's power the mighty-breasted,
    Who rules the billowy brine;
And, linked with golden Aphrodite.
The heavenly smith, in labour mighty,
    Grace matched with skill he sees;
And one that in his airy hand
Displayed a serpent-twisted wand,
    And floated on the breeze,
Both capped and shod with wings; and one
    That lay in sumptuous ease
On pillowed clouds, fair Semele's son,
    And quaffed the nectared bowl;
And one from whom the locks unshorn
Flowed like ripe fields of Autumn corn,
And beaming brightness, like the morn,
    Showered radiance on the pole;
And matron Juno's awful face;
And Dian, mistress of the chase;
And Pallas, that with eye of blue
Now sternly meets the hero's view
    Whom erst she met with love;

And, like a star of purer ray,
Apart, whom all the gods obey,
    The thunder-launching Jove.
The ravishment of such fair sight
Thrilled sense and soul with quick delight
    To bold Bellerophon:
Entranced he looked; his wingèd steed,
Dazed with the brightness, checked its speed,
    Nor more would venture on.
Deaf to the eager rider's call,
Who spurred to mount the Olympian wall,
    It stood like lifeless stone
A moment—then, with sudden wheel,
And headlong plunge, it 'gan to reel;
For awful now were heard to peal
    Sharp thunders from the pole,
And lightnings flashed, and darkly spread
O'er that rash rider's impious head,
    The sulphurous volumes roll.
With rapid gust the fiery storm
Resistless whirls his quaking form
    Down through the choking air.

Loud and more loud the thunders swell;
Him with blind speed the winds impel;
Three times three days and nights he
      fell
    Down through the choking air.
At length, in mazy terror lost,
Him the celestial courser tossed
    With fiercely-fretted mane;
And, by the close-involving blast
Impetuous hurried, he was cast
    On the Aleian plain.

XI.

Senseless, but lifeless not, he lay.
    The gods had mercy shown,
If they had slain, on that black day,
    The blasted Glaucus' son:
But all the gods conspired to hate
The man, with impious pride elate,
    Who dared to scale the sky.

Year after year, from that black day,
He pined his dreary life away,
Weak as a cloud or vapour grey,
    And vainly wished to die.
On a wide waste, without a tree,
The unfrequent traveller there might see
    The once great Glaucus' son.
Far from the haunts and from the
        tread
Of men, a joyless life he led ;
Less kin to living than to dead,
On folly's fruitage there he fed,
    With his blank self alone.
Even as a witless boy at school
Would sit and gaze into a pool
    The moody Glaucus' son,
Or to bring forth the blindworm red
That, creeping, loves a lightless bed,
    Would turn the old grey stone.
And thus he lived, and thus he died,
And ended to the brute allied,
    Who like a god began ;

And he hath gained a mournful fame,

And marred immortal praise with blame,

And taught to whoso names his name,

    PRIDE WAS NOT MADE FOR MAN!

1850.

IPHIGENIA.[5]

Λιτὰς δε καὶ κληδόνας πατρῴους
παρ' ουδὲν αἰῶνα παρθένειόν τ'
ἔθεντο φιλόμαχοι βραβῆς
φράσεν δ' ἀόζοις πατὴρ μετ' εὐχὰν
δίκαν χιμάιρας ὕπερθε βωμοῦ
πέπλοισι περιπετῆ
παντὶ θυμῷ προνωπῆ
λαβεῖν ἀέρδην στόματός τε καλλιπρώρου φυλακὰν κά-
      τασχεῖν
φθόγγον ἀραῖον οἴκοις.—ÆSCHYLUS.

THE ships are gathered in the bay,
   A thousand-masted army,
All eager for the Trojan fray,
   But the sky looks black and stormy.

From Strymon's shore, with surly roar,
   The Thracian blasts are blowing;
With fretted breast, and foamy crest,
   The adverse tide is flowing.

And Aulis' shore, so bright before,
   Is bleak, and grey, and dreary;
With dull delay, from day to day,
   The seamen's hearts are weary.
Dire omen to their ears the roar
   Of Jove's loud-rattling thunder;
The shivered sail, the shattered oar,
   The cable snapt in sunder.

What man is he that stands apart,
   In priestly guise long-vested,
Communing deep with his own heart,
   By sombre thoughts infested?
He hath a laurel in his hand,
   And on the dark storm gazing,
He broods, as he would understand
   The secret of its raising.

'Tis Calchas, whose divining mind
    The secret thought can follow
Of Jove, who shows to human kind
    His counsel by Apollo.
And they who trust in prophet's skill,
    On the lone rock have found him,
And throng, to learn the Supreme will,
    In eager crowds around him.

He stands; he looks, and reads the ground;
    He will nor see nor hear them;
But still they press, with swelling sound
    Of blameful murmurs, near him.
He goes; against a host in vain
    He plants his single freedom;
And to the tent o' the king of men
    With fretful force they lead him.

The Atridan stood without his tent,
    And scanned the welkin curiously,
If that the storm at length had spent
    Its gusty burden furiously.

Small help got he from cloud or sky,
　　From sad thoughts that oppressed him;
But blithe was his eye, when the seer came nigh,
　　And thus the king addressed him :—

"O son of Thestor! thou art wise,
　　Thou see'st what wintry weather
Scowls on our bright-faced enterprise,
　　And with a close-drawn tether
Holds us bound here against our will;
　　What cause doth so delay us?
Speak, sith thou hast a prophet's skill,
　　To me and Menelaus."

The seer was dumb; his fixed eye read
　　The insensate sand demurely;
"Nay, speak the truth," the Atridan said,
　　"For thou dost know it surely.
Thou need'st not fear the strong man's arm,
　　The king of men doth swear it,
Even by this kingly staff—no harm
　　Shall touch thee, while I bear it!"

F

The seer was dumb; the king was wroth:
    "Thou sellest dear thy prayers,
Thou sour-faced priest, and by my troth,
    Like thee are all soothsayers.
A mouthing and a mumping crew,
    With all things they will meddle;
And when they have made much ado,
    They speak a two-faced riddle!"

The seer was dumb.   "Nay, not for me,
    Stiff priest, for love of Hellas,
If Jove hath shown the truth to thee,
    Untie thy tongue and tell us.
If, in our sacred things, a vice
    Some god hath sore offended,
Declare, and, at a tenfold price,
    I vow it shall be mended.

"If fault there be in me or mine,
    Or in the chiefs the highest,
I will not swerve, but so incline
    As Jove shall point, unbiassed.

My crown, my wealth, my blood, my all,
   Myself and Menelaus,
Will give, if so we may recall
   The blasts that now delay us."

Then spake the prophet : " King, not well
   Apollo's priest thou chidest ;
But I the unwelcome truth will tell,
   And follow where thou guidest.
The best-loved stag of Dian thou
   Hast slain with evil arrow ;
Therefore this vengeful tempest now
   Consumes the Argive marrow.

" And thou, even thou, whose was the guilt,
   Must work the just atoning ;
When blood for blood is freely spilt,
   To joy will turn thy moaning.
If thou wilt ferry thee and thine
   Safe o'er the smooth-faced water,
Thou to the goddess must resign
   Blood of thy blood, thy daughter."

The monarch stood, and with his staff
    He smote the ground in sorrow;
Nor spake: the cup that he must quaff
    Is fire that burns his marrow.
No aid Laertes' son supplied,
    Nestor, or Menelaus;
For we must stay the winds, they cried,
    From Thrace, that so delay us.

And they have choked the father's prayer;
    And this their general will is,
To bring the maid, with promise fair
    To wed her to Achilles.
And they have sent a courier far
    To Argos steed-delighting,
And Clytemnestra reins the car,
    To answer their inviting.

And they have come in trim array,
    The mother and the daughter,
As hasting to a bridal gay
    Beside the briny water.

But, when they reach the Aulian strand,
　　No sight of gladness meets them;
Hushed lies the camp; with outstretched hand
　　No forward father greets them.

And she is led, the daughter fair,
　　By will that may not falter,
Where priests a sacrifice prepare
　　For Dian's gloomy altar;
Where Calchas stands with folded hands,
　　And dense beholders gather;
And with grief bent, on a plane-tree leant
　　With backward gaze, her father.

Ah, woe is me! and can it be,
　　That, with sharp knife, thou darest
Strike such a neck, and forceful break
　　This flower thy first and fairest?
Will he not hear, her father dear,
　　When her shrill plaint she poureth;
Nor Jove above look down in love,
　　When guiltless youth imploreth?

She stretched her hands to the standers by,
　And tenderly besought them;
With shafts of pity from her eye,
　The lovely maiden smote them.
O! like a picture to be seen
　Was she, so chaste and beautiful,
And to her father's will had been
　In all so meek and dutiful.

How often, at his kingly board,
　With filial heart devoted,
To grace the banquet, she had poured
　The mellow lay clear-throated!
But now that voice shall sing no more;
　They gag her mouth, lest, dying,
A curse on Argos she should pour,
　With evil-omened crying.

And, as stern Calchas gives behest,
　They with a cord have bound her;
And she hath wrapt her saffron vest
　In decent folds around her.

And as a kid supine is laid,
　　They on the altar lay her;
As bleeds a kid, so bleeds the maid,
　　To the knife o' the priestly slayer.

But a weight is rolled from the heart of Greece,
　　And the clouds from the sky are driven;
And the sun looks down with an eye of peace
　　From the fresh blue face of heaven.
The westering breeze the seamen hailed,
　　That smoothed the Ægean water;
But with sad heart the monarch sailed,
　　For he had lost a daughter.

WAIL OF AN IDOL.[6]

Μὴ δή μοι θάνατόν γε παραύδα, φαίδιμ' Ὀδυσσεῦ·
Βουλοίμην κ' ἐπάρουρος ἐὼν θητευέμεν ἄλλῳ,
Ἀνδρὶ παρ' ἀκλήρῳ, ᾧ μὴ βίοτος πολὺς εἴη,
Ἢ πᾶσιν νεκύεσσι καταφθιμένοισιν ἀνάσσειν.—HOMER.

O DREARY, dreary shades !
O sad and sunless glades !
O yellow, yellow meads
    Of asphodel !
Where the dream-like idol strays,
On lone and lifeless ways,
Through Hades' weary maze,
    And sings his own sad knell.

O sullen, solemn, silent clime !
O lazy pace of noiseless time !

O where is the blythe and gamesome change
   Of the many-nurturing earth?
   The dance of joy, the flush of mirth,
Life's vast and varied range?

O dreary, dreary vales!
O heavy, heavy gales!
Fraught with the dreamy dew of sleep,
Over the joyless fields ye sweep;
O sullen, sullen, streaky sky,
Where the changeless moon, with a leaden eye,
   Aloft hangs languidly,
And yellow vapours mount up high,
And flickering lights in a wild dance fly,
Like the last fleet flash when the strangled die,
Shooting across the darkling eye.

   O sullen, sullen sky!
  Where the brown bat wings,
  And the lone bird sings
A chant like the chant of death;

While sad souls wake

The stagnant lake

With a sobbing, struggling breath.

O sad, O sad is the wail of the stream,

Mingling its sighs with the dead man's dream ;

Winding, winding nine times round,

Weary, wandering, 'scapeless bound !

And the black, black kine,

In lazy ranks,

Are cropping the sickly herb

From the reedy Stygian banks ;

And hissing things,

With poisoned blood,

Are crawling through the bubbling mud.

O sad, O sad is the endless row

Of poplars black ; oh, sad and slow

Is the long-drawn train of the sons of woe,

The silent-marching ghosts !

And they share no more in the feast of glee,

And the dance, and the song, and the wine-cup free ;

Where the bard divine, with mellow lays,

Is singing the gods' and the heroes' praise ;

And they share no more
Loud laughter's roar,
The silent-marching ghosts !
I hear their cry,
As they flit swift by
On noiseless wing,
Hurrying through the wide outspread
Gates that gape for the countless dead :
I hear the cry
Of the wailing ghosts ;
Their voices small,
Like a drowning thing,
Drawn echoless along the long dim hall ;
And some are whirled,
In the mighty void,
Like a leaf in the gurgling tide
And some are hurled,
With a gusty fit,
Into the deep Tartarean pit ;
And some do sway,
Like a blind thing stray,
To and fro in the pathless air ;

And some, whom chance less stormy
  rules,
Sit sipping the blood from crimson pools.

O sad is the throne,
Dark, drear, alone,
Of the stern, relentless pair!
With gloom enveiled,
In judgment mailed,
A joyless sway they bear.
No circling years,
No sounding spheres,
No hopes and fears,
  Are there;
They sit on the throne,
Dark, drear, alone,
A stern relentless pair.
And beside them sits
A monster dire,
Watching the darkness with eyes of fire,
The dog of the triform head;
And his harsh bark splits,
Like thunder fits,

The realm of the silent dead.

    Oh, sad is the throne,

    Dark, drear, alone,

Of the stern, relentless pair !

    O dreary, dreary shades !

    O sad and sunless glades !

    O yellow, yellow meads

      Of asphodel !

    O loveless, joyless homes !

    O weary, starless domes !

Where the wind-swept idol roams,

    And sighs his own sad knell.

    O sullen, solemn, silent clime !

    O lazy pace of noiseless time !

O where are the many-coloured joys of earth ?

O where is the loud strong voice of mirth ?

    The jubilant shout,

    Of the light-heeled rout,

Where the dance is whirling about and about ;

    The roving joy

    Of the bright-faced boy,

When he plays with life as he plays with a toy.

O where is the change
　　Of joy and woe?
The love of friend,
　　The hate of foe?
O where is the bustle of many-winged life,
And of man with man the many-mingling strife?
　　Where to live was to fight,
　　And to fight was delight,
Where the fair face smiled on the strong-armed
　　knight.
　　O Hermes! leader of the dead,
　　　　Thou wingèd god
　　　　Of the golden rod,
　　O lead me, lead me further still!
Lead me to Lethe's silent stream,
　　That I may drink, deep drink my fill,
And wash from my soul this long life-dream!
　　O lead me, lead me to Lethe's shore,
　　Where Memory lives no more!

ARIADNE.[7]

Χρυσοκόμης δε Διάνυσος ξανθὴν Ἀριάδνην
κόυρην Μίνωος, θαλερὴν ποιήσατ᾽ ἄκοιτιν
τὴν τὲ οἱ ἀθάνατον καὶ ἀγήρω θῆκε Κρονίων.—HESIOD.

" Protinus adspicies venienti nocte coronam
  Gnossida ; Theseo crimine facta dea est."—OVID.

I.

ARIADNE, Ariadne,
Thou art left alone, alone !
And the son of Attic Aegeus,
Faithless Theseus, he is flown.
Ariadne, Ariadne,
In a sea-cave left she sleepeth ;
In her dreams her bosom heaveth,
Through her dreams the maiden weepeth.

With an ugly dream she struggles;
In the bright and sunny weather,
O'er the meadows green and flowery,
She and Theseus walk together.

Suddenly there sweeps a change;
O'er a moor of hard brown heather,
O'er a bare and treeless waste,
She and Theseus walk together.

Cold and loveless is the air,
Huge white mists are trailing near her:
And the fitful swelling blast
Pipes with shrill note clear and clearer.

By an old grey tower she stands,
Where the ruin starts and crumbles;
Wandering by a lone black lake,
On a cold grey stone she stumbles.

"Theseus! Theseus!"—to his arms
Close she clings; but like a trailing
Mist he flees; and o'er the waste
Laughter answers to her wailing.

Dim confusion blinds her eye,
Through her veins the chilly horror

Shoots : she stands ; she looks ; she runs
O'er the moor with mazy error.
And she screams, with rending cries,
" Save me, Jove, save Ariadne !
Theseus, Theseus, in the waste
Hast thou left thy Ariadne ?"
And the Spirits of the storm
Shout around her—" Ariadne !
Thou art left alone, alone,
In the waste, O Ariadne ! "

II.

From the painful dream she wakes,
Starts, and looks, and feels for Theseus ;
On the cold rock-floor her hand
Falls, and feels in vain for Theseus.
" Theseus, Theseus ! "—he is gone ;
Dost thou see that full sail swelling ?
There he hies, with rapid keel,
Soon to find his Attic dwelling.

"Theseus! Theseus!"—she doth beat
The breasted wave with idle screaming.
Like a white sea-bird so small,
Now his distant sail is gleaming:
Now 'tis vanished.   O'er the isle
Hurries vagrant Ariadne;
None she sees, and, when she calls,
Answers none to Ariadne.
'Neath a high-arched rock she rests,
Weary, and, with meek behaviour,
Stretched upon a stony floor,
Plains her prayer to Jove the Saviour :—

    Mighty Jove, strong to destroy,
        Stronger to save,
    Hear; nor in vain may Minos' daughter
        Thy mercy crave !
    Weak is a maiden's wit: I saw
        The galliard stranger,
    And, with wise clue, I brought him through
        The mazy danger.
    My father's halls I left; I gave
        My heart's surrender;

He loved the flower, and plucked the fruit,
 With hand untender.
Mighty Jove, the suppliant's friend,
 My supplication
Hear thou, and touch my prostrate woe
 With restoration!
She spake; and, on the stony floor,
Stretched she lay in tearful sorrow;
Slumber, sent from Saviour Jove,
Bound her gently till the morrow.

III.

Wake, Ariadne!
Wake from thy slumbers;
Wake with new heart,
Which no sorrow encumbers!
Black Night is away now,
And glorious Day now
 Reddens apace.
The white mists are fleeing,
And o'er the Ægean,

His shining steeds follow
The call of Apollo,
　　And snort for the race.
Hark ! through thy slumbers,
Undulant numbers
　　Quicken the air !
O'er the Ægean
Swells the loud pæan
　　With melody rare ;
The clear-throated flute,
And the sweet-sounding lute,
The cymbals' shrill jangle,
And tinkling triangle,
　　And tambour, are there.
Wake, Ariadne !
Look through thy slumbers !
The Mænads, to meet thee,
Marshal their numbers.
Down, from the sky
Dionysus has sent them ;
Rosiest beauty
Venus has lent them.

Hovering nigh,
Their thin robes floating,
With balm in their eye,
Thy wounds they are noting,
  O Ariadne!
Blest be the bride
(So echoes their song)
That shall sleep by the side
Of the wine-god strong,
  Fair Ariadne!
Daughter of Minos,
A mortal betrays thee,
But a god for his bride
To Olympus shall raise thee!
Like a gem thou shalt shine
'Mid the bright starry glory;
A name shall be thine
With the famous in story.
Wake, Ariadne,
From Earth's heavy slumbers;
Wake to new life,
Which no sorrow encumbers!

IV.

Ariadne from her slumber
Woke and rose, and smiled benignly,
Radiant from the rapturous dreams
That stirred her inmost soul divinely.
Round her stood the Mænad maids,
Round her swelled their tuneful chorus;
Round her wheeled their floating dance,
To a piping reed sonorous.
With them wheeled a prick-eared crew,
Hairy-limbed, with goatish features;
Pans and Satyrs strange to view,
Forest-haunting, freakish creatures.
Old Silenus, bald and broad,
Stood beside, his bright face showing
Ploughed with laughter; his full eye
Brimmed with mirth to overflowing.
Strange; but Ariadne saw,
With broad eyes, a sight yet stranger;
Troops of shaggy forest whelps
Thronged around, and brought no danger.

Bearded goat, and tusky boar,
Fox that feasts on stealthy slaughter,
Tawny lion, tiger fierce,
Harmless looked on Minos' daughter.
Lo ! a spotted pard appears
At the feet of Ariadne ;
Comes, and, like a prayerful child,
Kneels before thee, Ariadne.
Pleased the savage brute she sees
Stretch its brindled length demurely ;
Mounts the offered seat, and rides
On the panther's back securely.
Forward now the spotted pard
Moves with measured pace and wary ;
Then aloft (O wonder strange !)
Paws the heavenward pathway airy.
Fear thee not, thou Gnossian maid,
Gods are with thee where thou fliest ;
Dionysus waits for thee,
Near the throne of Jove the Highest.
In Olympus' azure dells,
Waits the god in ivy bowers,

Where for thee immortal Hebe
Twines the amaranthine flowers;
Where the purple bowl of joy
Brims for thee; where bitter sorrow
Grows not; where to-day's keen thrill
Leaves no languid throb to-morrow.
Flourish there, immortal bride,
In sculptor's stone and minstrel's story;
Shine, to sorrowing hearts a sign,
High amid the starry glory!

GALATEA.

Δωρὶς καὶ Πανόπη καὶ εὐειδὴς Γαλάτεια.—HESIOD.

I.

Hast heard the ancient story,
   The worthy old Greek theme
Of lovely Galatea
   And ugly Polypheme?
It is a tale of sadness,
   As many tales there be:
Attend, and I will tell it,
   As it was told to me.
There lived a heathen giant
   In ancient Sicily,
A son of strong Poseidon,
   Who rules the stormy sea;

A huge unsightly monster;
   Beneath his shaggy hair
(So learnèd Virgil sayeth),
   One big round eye did stare.
His trunk was like a huge tree
   Dug from an old brown moss;
His skin was hard and horny,
   Like a stiff rhinoceros.
On bloody food he feasted;
   As ancient tales relate,
Each blessed day to supper
   Two living men he ate,
A score of goats' milk cheeses,—
   And, mingled with black gore,
Red wine he drank in rivers,
   Till he could drink no more.
This monster loved with hot love
   (That such a thing should be!)
The lovely Galatea,
   A daughter of the sea.
His love he plied full stoutly;
   He fell upon his knees,

And swore she might command him
 In all that she should please.
He filled the seas with weeping;
 His big round eye was red;
His hair he tore like forests
 From off his clumsy head.
He beat his breast—by Neptune
 He swore, and with wild nails
Digged his rude cheeks; and Ætna
 Re-echoed with his wails.
But the maid was cold as marble,
 She would nor see nor hear;
And shrank with fear and loathing
 When his brutish bulk came near.
" What shall I do ? " quoth Cyclops;
 " This sin she shall atone:
Me shall she scout ?—a sea-girl
 Strong Neptune's son disown ? "
He asked advice of Proteus;
 Old Proteus said, " Behold !
I change myself; but can I
 Change thy lead into gold ? "

He asked advice of Nereus :
   The hoary god appeared ;
He could not give the monster
   His own white snowy beard,
The beard that charmed young Doris
   More than mad Triton's eye,
But Nereus had an eye, too,
   Of calm blue prophecy.
Quoth Nereus, "Son of Neptune,
   If thou wilt win her love,
Eat not the flesh of mortals,
   Revere the name of Jove :—
And yet thy case is hopeless,
   Even wert thou free from blame,—
She loves a gentle shepherd,
   And Acis is his name."
He spake : the Cyclops bellowed,
   And, like a cloven rock,
His monstrous jaws were sundered ;
   Earth trembled at the shock.
Quoth he, " By Father Neptune,
   It will be wondrous strange

If this same piping shepherd
   Oust me—I vow revenge ! "
And Ocean from his blue depths
   Replied, " It will be strange ! "
And from their hollow caverns
   The rocks replied—" Revenge ! "

II.

It was an hour of stillness,
   In the green and leafy June,
Midway between the cool eve
   And the sultry ray of noon.
Thin clouds were floating idly,
   And with his changing rays
The playful sun bedappled
   The green and ferny braes.
The birds were chirping faintly,
   It scarcely was a song ;
But the breath of green creation
   And fragrant life was strong.

The lazy trees were nodding,
　　The flowers were half awake,
And toilsome men were basking,
　　Like the serpent in the brake.
The Borean winds were sleeping,
　　Asleep was ocean's roar,
And ripple was chasing ripple
　　On the silver-sounding shore.
The countless ocean-daughters
　　Were weaving from the waves
Bright webs of scattered sunlight
　　To deck their sparry caves ;
And in her sapphire chamber,
　　Of lucent beauty rare,
The sea-queen Amphitrite
　　Was plaiting her sea-green hair.
But the chase, and the dance, and the gambol,
　　And the tramp of Triton war
Were dumb—for father Neptune
　　Had reined his billowy car.
The lovely Galatea,
　　Within a silent bay,

With her dear shepherd Acis
   In blest seclusion lay. ,
High craggy rocks steep-rising,
   The bosomed beach enclose;
And at the feet of the goddess
   The rippling wavelet flows.
The shepherd sang to please her:
   He piped a simple air,
And as he sang gazed alway
   Into that face so fair;
He drank the dew of heaven,
   Deep draughts of beauty rare,
And he never could weary gazing
   On the face of the sea-nymph fair.
He sang the shepherd of Latmos,
   Endymion the blest;
He sang his sweet day labours,
   And his sweeter night of rest:
His labours sweet and easy,
   Beneath the sunny cope,
To watch the fleecy wanderers
   That cropped the Carian slope;

His rest more sweet, when Dian,
   Fleet huntress of the woods,
Came bounding over the mountains,
   Came leaping over the floods,
Came dancing over the rivers,
   That with her beauty shone,
To see in mellow moonlight
   The sleep of Endymion.

She looked on the lovely sleeper,
   The soul that knew no strife;
He looked like some spotless marble
   God-wakened into life.

She bended gently o'er him;
   Beneath his breast of snow,
She heard the pure blood flowing,
   So musical below.

She smoothed the mossy pillow
   All softly where he slept,
And a fragrant flower sprang near him,
   Each tear the goddess wept.

She kissed his cheeks so downy,
   So beautiful, so brown,

And amid his locks so golden
   She wove a silver crown.
Her breath was music round him,
   And her presence fancies fair,
That cradled the happy dreamer
   In a winged and rosy lair.
She looked on the sleeping shepherd,
   And her love with gazing grew,
And the limbs of the lovely mortal
   She bathed in immortal dew.
O happy shepherd of Latmos,
   What sleeping bliss divine!
I might close mine eyes for ever,
   To win one sleep like thine!
Thus sang the gentle Acis,
   And rose to pluck a bloom,
With the hair of the lovely sea-nymph
   To mingle its sweet perfume.
A noise was heard—a rumbling,
   A crashing sound.—"Oh stay!
O Acis, Acis!"—Buried
   Beneath a rock he lay.

The rock came from the high cliff,
    A huge and pointed stone,
By the hand of the savage monster,
    The bloody Cyclops, thrown.
He stood on the craggy coping,
    And laughed with a laughter wild ;
" I have slain at once, and buried,
    False goddess, thy mortal child ! "
The lovely Galatea,
    She fell in speechless woe ;
On the rock that covered her Acis
    Her tears unceasing flow.

THE JUDGMENT OF PARIS.

ἐκρίθη δ ἔρις ἃν ἐν Ἴδᾳ
κρίνει τρίσσας μακάρων
παῖδας ἀνὴρ βούτας
ἐπὶ δορὶ καὶ φόνῳ καὶ ἐμῶν μελάθρων λώβᾳ·
στένει δὲ καὶ τις ἀμφὶ τὸν εὔρουν Εὐρώταν
Δάκαινα πολυδάκρυτος ἐν δόμοις κόρα,
πολιὸν δ ἐπὶ κρᾶτα μάτηρ
τέκνων θανόντων τίθεται χέρα
δρύπτεταί τε παρειὰν
δίαιμον ὄνυχα τιθεμένα σπαραγμοῖς.
—EURIPIDES.

I.

On lofty Ida's grassy slope
    Sat Priam's shepherd son,
What time Apollo's beaming car
    Its course had wellnigh run,

One radiant day in June.   He leant
   Upon his curvèd crook,
Musing; and to the sky around,
And to the various-dappled ground,
And the slow-oozing mossy rill,
On the green bosom of the hill,
   Sent many a wandering look.
And with intenter gaze he eyed
The palace of his father's pride,
   That in the vale below
Rose regal; battlement and tower
And massy porch of brazen power
   To stay the battering foe:
And many a dwelling sheltered well,
'Neath Ilium's sacred citadel
Far-smoking; and the firm-faced line
   Of the high-gated wall,
That rose with upright strength divine,
   At strong Poseidon's call.
And in his heart the hopeful thought
Swelled venturous; and fair fancies
    float

Before him; and the secret germ
Of manhood's ripening fate grew warm.
The pomp of life in rolling splendour,
   Bright wealth and purple power,
And rosy smiles and twinings tender,
   In love's fresh-blossoming hour
O'ercame his spirit, and possessed
With pleasant tumult his young breast.
Thus finely rapt, he mused, and leant
   Upon his curvèd crook;
And, as the shadows came and went,
Upon the hill, he, like a seer,
Saw flitting shapes of hope and fear,
   In the heart's shadowy book.

II.

Serene and still the sun doth set,
   The wave with gold is gleaming;
But see a glory brighter yet
   From high Olympus streaming!

The shepherd lifts his eye, and looks :
   A splendour like a star
Sails westward ; like a watch-fire now—
   Now 'tis a flaming car.
O Heavens ! what glorious sight he sees !
   With sweep of breezy lightness
Down Ida's slope the car descends,
   And fills the mount with brightness ;
Then lights at Paris' foot.   The god
That bears a serpent-cinctured rod,
And guides, a wingèd charioteer,
That radiant cloud-car's swift career,
Checks the keen steeds with cunning rein,
And thus bespeaks the princely swain :
" Beautiful son of Ilium's king,
To thee from Jove on flaming wing
This word I bring : A contest rare,
Which is the fairest of the three,
Between Jove's daughter and his wife
And Aphrodite golden-fair
Breaks Heaven's sweet peace.   Great Jove
    to thee

The judgment yields.   This hour prepare
   Thy doom to end the strife."
He spake ; and forth from out the cloud
That doth the Olympian car enshroud,
Steps lofty Hera, with the mien
And posture of a queen.
" Shepherd, thou seest the Queen of Heaven,
   Jove's thunder-hall is mine,
To me if beauty's prize be given,
   Attend what meed is thine.
I give thee sway and lordly rule ;
   This populous Asian land
Shall be to thee a training school,
   To mould with plastic hand
  The pliant millions of mankind ;
   Thy lofty thought shall be
 A law to ages, that resigned
   Shall take their stamp from thee.
Where to Apollo swells the pæan,
From the bright isles of the Ægean—
Where the white peaks of Caucasus shine
O'er the dark Euxine's horrent brine—

Where blest Arabia's sunny shore
Teems with the fragrant spicy store—
Where Ganges rolls his ample flood,
And spreads wide leagues of pregnant mud,
Far as the wine-god tiger-borne
Travelled the bright realms of the morn ;
So far, if beauty's prize be mine,
Shall wealth, and state, and power be thine."
She spake ; and her proud form back drew
Into the cloud ; when forth with spear,
And casque, and large round buckler clear,
Jove's blue-eyed daughter stept to view.
" Thou seest the warrior-maid of Heaven,
    The strength of spears is mine,
To me if beauty's prize be given,
    The hero's fame is thine.
I give the strength of sinewy arm,
    And the sure-levelled blow,
To stay the march of haughty harm,
    And lay the lawless low.
The daring thought, the piercing eye,
    The free and fearless breath,

The grasp that snatches victory
   Even in the throat of death.
Where forests of the threatful spear
Flash o'er the line from van to rear;
Where furious Mars in scythèd car
Leads the hot chase of panting war;
Where quakes the air with arrowy storm,
And man to man works mortal harm,
Thou shalt not fear; but to the cry
Of freedom, and of fatherland,
Shalt feel thy manhood mounting high,
And, with a chosen true-sworn band,
Breasting wars crimson tide shalt stand
Firm as a rooted tree. Thy name
Shall be a charm to smother shame,
A travelling watchword to the free;
The peasant's song shall tell of thee,
And little children shout for glee;
The hearth by thee shall blaze more brightly,
And loving hearts shall beat more lightly;
Thou shalt be blest of mothers; thou
Shalt see the ploughman turn his plough

O'er fields of recent slaughter;
The full-eared corn shall wave its pride,
Where wisdom was true valour's guide,
  From me, Jove's blue-eyed daughter."
She spake; and back the maid withdrew;
  When forth, in beauty mighty,
Stept radiant to the ravished view
  The golden Aphrodite.
"Shepherd, the strongest power in Heaven,
  All-conquering love, is mine;
To me if beauty's prize be given,
  Earth's fairest fair is thine.
I give thee beauty; being fair,
  A fairer thou shalt find,
And mated live the loveliest pair,
  From Gaul to furthest Ind.
The clear smooth brow, the glowing eye,
  The shining hue of health,
The living grace that none may buy
  With mines of golden wealth,
I give to thee.   In fragrant beds,
Where violets nod their purple heads,

Where odorous jessamine and roses
Twine the cool bower where peace reposes,
Where glimpses of the stray sunshine,
Pierce the broad-leaved dark-clustered vine ;
There thou shalt look in beauty's face,
And gently twine the soft embrace,
Till thy full liquid eye shall swim
With ecstasy, and overbrim
Thy soul with joy, and every limb
Thrill with rare transport.   Gods above
No keener joy have known than love,
Than when with impulse fresh and mighty,
It stirs the soul and elevates,
And every throbbing sense dilates,
By gift of golden Aphrodite.
Such bliss, if beauty's prize be mine,
Shepherd of Ida, shall be thine."
She spake ; and the full-floating view
Of her bright fairness overthrew
All sterner purpose.   " Thou art fair,"
He cried, " beyond the dull compare
Of meaner forms !   Henceforth my duty,

With fervid heart-resolve, shall be
To win the fair, and worship beauty
In thee, and those most like to thee."
He said ; and straight the vision flew,
Dissolving from his tranceful view,
   And all the air was clear.
A wonder-stricken wight he stood,
Like poet, when in tranceful mood
   He feels the Muses near ;
But, as he homeward bent his way,
'Neath the last streaks of rosy day,
Jove's thunder from the hill-top grey
   Rolled ominous on his ear.

THESEUS.[8]

Θησεὺς εἰς τὴν νῦν πόλιν οὖσαν
ξυνῴκισε πάντας καὶ ἠνάγκασε
μιᾷ πόλει ταύτῃ χρῆσθαι.—THUCYDIDES.

I.

'Tis the eighth of Pyanepsion,
    The vintage-time is o'er,
And the Attic crowds are thronging
    To the bright Phalerian shore.
From the shrine of Dionysus,
    In the city, forth they fare,
And wave the green vine-branches
    In the breezy morning air.
Old men, and maids, and matrons,
    From household labour free,
And working men, red-bonneted,
    And boys with noisy glee.

The noble and the ploughman,
  The freeman and the slave,
In festal march commingling,
  The viny branches wave.
And ever, as they march along,
  They raise their blithe halloo,
And shout the name of Theseus,
  With 'Ἰοῦ ἰοῦ ἰοῦ.
"O son of Ægeus, fetched at last,
  Across the briny foam,
We welcome thee, again to see
  Thy long-lost Attic home!"
And some with godlike Theseus' name
  The gallant Cimon join,
Who brought the bones of Ægeus' son
  Across the foamy brine:
"O Cimon, gallant Cimon,
  Thou o'er the watery track
From the wild men of Scyros
  Didst win our hero back!"
And thus they sing, and thus they march,
  And like a stream they pour,

Until with swelling bands they come
  To the bright Phalerian shore.

II.

Lift up thine eyes, and know them,
  In festal broad display,
The Attic tribes all camped around
  The bright Phalerian bay.
I see the well-bronzed mountaineers,
  The stout Acharnian blades,
Who hew the tree, and char the wood
  In Parnes' piny glades;
The men who watch on Phyle,
  Proud neighbours of the sky,
And look o'er all the Attic plain
  From rocky fortress high;
Who dwell on Corydallus,
  To Theseus' memory true,
For there the grim Procrustes
  That godlike hero slew;
The sailors of Piraeus,
  Where rests on rocky pillow

Lord of the seas, Themistocles,
   Beside the briny billow;
From verdant Cerameicus,
   Where sacred olives grow,
And sculptured stones and cypress-trees
   The sleeping heroes show;
The youths of the Lyceum,
   With light-heeled step elastic,
To every manly posture trained
   By noble art gymnastic;
The men of white Colonus,
   Where the awful Furies reign,
And Poseidon horse careering shows
   The mace that rules the main.
The people of Eleusis,
   Where the mystic goddess dwells;
The Rharian plain and Rheti,
   Where the briny fountain wells.
The men of Marathon I see,
   Brave men with welcome harsh,
Who met the Mede, and him with speed
   Drave through the blood-stained marsh

Back to the fretful sea.   With them
   The men of Rhamnus stand,
Who, from the rock of Nemesis look
   On the peaked Eubœan land ;
Then Brauron's priestly choir, whose hands
   Have holy service done
To Dian's idol bravely filched
   By Agamemnon's son
From Tauris' scowling shores ; then they
   From Laurium's rocky store
Who win from the harsh-grained mountain's bowels
   The pliant silver ore.
And on the extreme beach I see
   The men of the Sunian strand,
From the high-perched shrine of the maid divine,
   With the strong spear-shaking hand
Who welcomes the storm-vext sailor back
   To his dear-loved Attic land.
Oh, fair to see on the storied ground
   Is the festive pomp to-day
Of the Attic tribes all camped around
   The bright Phalerian bay !

III.

'Ιοῦ, ἰοῦ along the shore,
   'Ιοῦ among the hills,
'Ιοῦ, ἰοῦ the billowy blue
   Of the bright Phalerum fills !
'Ιοῦ, 'Ιοῦ the gay trireme
   Of the gallant Cimon nears ;
The pennons glitter in the sun,
   The lusty seaman cheers.
And now they hale the ships ashore ;
   Now on the mole they stand,
The captains, and the admiral
   Who holds the high command.
" Jove bless thee, gallant Cimon ! "
   For thus they sing and say ;
" Thou bring'st the bones of Theseus
   To Theseus' home to-day.
Thou tall and handsome Cimon,
   Brave, generous, and gay ;
The gods do for thee even more
   Than thou for us this day ! "

A fair and noble convoy
   Now on the shore behold
Around the bier of Theseus,
   That kingly hero old :
The high priest of Eleusis,
   With purple tunic dight,
And round his brow a fillet bound
   Of pure and spotless white ;
The archon king, with myrtle bound,
   The archon of the year,
The polemarch and thesmothetes,
   Around great Theseus' bier ;
The pilots of the public weal,
   Free counsellors of the Free,
That watch the spark o' the sleepless fire,
   And frame the wise decree ;
The judges of the hill of Mars
   With reverend pomp are there,
That by the awful Furies' shrine
   The doom of blood declare.
Then all the mingled people,
   The freeman and the slave,

Around the bier of Theseus
    Their viny branches wave;
Old men, and maids, and matrons,
    From household labour free;
And working men, red-bonneted,
    And boys with noisy glee.
And then in banded ranks they form,
    And in festive lines they go,
To the city of Athena,
    Where the sacred olives grow;
And ever as they wind along,
    With measured pomp decorous,
From rank to rank well varied swells
    The mellow-throated chorus.

CHORUS OF YOUNG MEN.

1.

The son of old Ægeus was valiant and brave!
    From the near Trœzenian strand
He scorned to return o'er the smooth-flowing wave,
    To his home in the dear Attic land;

But over the mountains craggy and high,
Where the wild winds rave, and the dark clouds
      fly,
Where the fierce-hearted chief of the plundering
      clan
Lies in wait for the life of the wayfaring man :
    There, there, and only there,
    Would godlike Theseus go.

2.

Where leech Æsculapius brooks his skill
   In the famed Epidaurian land,
Stood huge Periphetes, grim lord of the hill,
   With a brazen club in his hand.
Him where the pass with his bulk he bestrode,
Strong Theseus laid stark all his length on the
      road ;
And his big brazen club for a trophy he bore,
As the hide of the lion strong Hercules wore :
    There, there, breathless there,
    He laid the monster low.

3.

Near Corinth, that looks east and west to the
    sea,
  Lived Sinis, the godless offender,
Who tore the stout limbs that were tied to the
    tree
  By the strength of the savage pine-bender.
Him Theseus grasps, and his huge limbs he joins
With cords to a brace of well-bended pines;
Then, freed with a jerk, the trees fly to heaven,
And limb from limb is asunder riven:
    There, there, the birds in the air
    His quivering body tore.

4.

In Megaris Sciron kept his lair,
  On the rocks beside the sea;
No harmless wayfarer did Sciron spare
  On the rocks beside the sea.
"Come wash my feet, good stranger mine!"
And he kicked him into the billowy brine.

Mercy shall none to the merciless be.
Over the cliff and into the sea,

    Theseus flung his huge hulk there,
    To bleach on the stony shore!

5.

Beneath Corydallus Procrustes dwelt,
    The life of the lawless he led;
His torturing force the traveller felt,
    Being racked on an iron bed.
Beneath Corydallus, in the hollow,
Theseus prayed to the archer Apollo;
Then gashed his brow with a blow unsightly,
And lopped his legs, and stretched him tightly:

    "There, there, sleep on the lair
    Which thine own blood made gory!"

6.

The son of old Ægeus was valiant and brave;
    The sons of Pallas were banded,
Fifty foes with glittering glaive,
    But he smote them single-handed.

Over the brow of the flowery Hymettus,
Through the midland, by blooming Gargettus,
Circling they came with a bristling array,
As hunters the stag when he stands at bay;
　　But there, there, he smote them there,
　　And his name shall be famous in story.

CHORUS OF YOUNG MAIDENS.

1.

Didst thou hear the voice of woe,
　　Cries of woe and wailing,
Lifted hands and tearful flow
　　O'er the land prevailing?
'Tis come! 'tis come! the year that shames
　　The humbled Attic nation;
'Tis come! the black, black hour that claims
　　The monstrous immolation.
Seven sires must send their sons,
　　And seven dames their daughters,
The ripest and the loveliest ones,
　　Across the Cretan waters.

Minos there, who lords the deep,
  With fate shall overpower them,
And in his darksome-winding keep
  The Minotaur devour them.
Woe! woe! the year of blood!
  The day of desolation!
When sorrow streameth like a flood
  O'er all the Attic nation!

2.

The lot, the lot, the bloody lot!
  But why this dinsome cheering?
'Tis he! 'tis he! Greek mothers, see
  The kingly youth appearing!
The noble Theseus! he hath heard
  What blameful words do gather
Among the people blindly stirred
  Against his grey-haired father;
And he hath thought a kingly thing;
  To stay the rude commotion
Himself before the Fate will fling
  Himself with high devotion.

His blood the king's own son shall pour,
   And share his people's slaughter,
Or he will slay the Minotaur
   Across the Cretan water.
Bless thee ! bless thee ! noble youth !
   The gods shall help thy daring ;
Return again, in thy white train
   The bright redemption bearing !

3.

The summer's sultry heat is gone,
   The fresh sea-breeze is blowing ;
'Tis the feast of Pyanepsion,
   And the sweet new wine is glowing.
A cheer—a cheer across the main !
   A shout comes from the billow !
Theseus, Theseus comes again ;
   Shake sorrow from your pillow !
No more, ye fathers, mourn your sons !
   Mothers, weep not your daughters !
He brings you back your dear-loved ones
   Across the Cretan waters.

From the trunk with trenchant glaive
    The monster's head he severed,
The mazes of the darksome cave
    With prudent clue recovered.
Welcome to thy country's shore,
    Thou king's son girt with glory;
And live in song for evermore
    The pride of Attic story!

CHORUS OF OLD MEN.

1.

Wise was the man, most wise,
Who first with cunning-thoughted phrase declared
    That earth and glowing skies
Were by the might of primal Jove prepared.
    Jove, first of gods, arose
From the chaotic sluggish Night inform;
    And lo! the dense dark glows
Forthwith, as the strong sunshine breaks the storm.

By Jove the starry spheres
Were fired; by Jove the bright-eyed flowers peeped
    forth,
    And all the pomp appears
Of various-pulsing life that treads the jocund earth.

2.

    This Theseus knew; and when
His ordering eye scanned the tumultuous life
    Of the old Attic men,
By love's strong bond he quelled the unholy strife.
    The ploughman of the plain,
The mountain shepherd, and rough seaman flock
    To own the social rein
Swayed by his hand from the Cecropian rock.
    No more doth glen with glen
Hold feud; the soil reeks not with kindred
    slaughter;
    And all the Attic men
Love the Athenian maid, great Jove's strong-hearted
    daughter.

CHORUS OF POOR PEOPLE.

1.

Oh, hard is the poor man's lot on earth !
 The rich man like a god
Rides through the sky, careering high ;
 The poor man cleaves the clod.
Bent o'er the clay from day to day,
 He is grey before his prime ;
And with aching bones beneath the stones
 He is laid before his time.

2.

The rich man is lord of the heathy hills ;
 He is king of the grassy plains,
Without a thought his chest he fills,
 And counts his careless gains.
The poor for him sore burdens bear,
 And in dark mines they burrow ;
But he hath more care for a stag or a hare,
 Than for all the poor man's sorrow.

3.

But Theseus was the poor man's friend,
   He felt their sore disaster,
He taught the proud man's will to bend;
   The strong man found a master.
And equal law from him they sought,
   The great and eke the small;
The noble for his faction fought,
   The monarch stood for all.

4.

Oh, hard is the poor man's lot on earth!
   But when the just man reigns,
A cheerful blaze shines from his hearth
   That lightens all his pains.
O saviour Jove! to earth still send
   —This hope from thee we borrow—
Some champion bold, like Theseus old,
   To heal the poor man's sorrow.

IV.

And thus they sang, and thus they marched,
  Till they reached Ilissus' water,
And to the god-loved city came
  Of Jove's spear-shaking daughter.
Beneath the awful hill of Mars,
  Where blood for blood atones,
A gently swelling knoll receives
  The godlike hero's bones.
And round the bier the people throng
  With reverent circling ring,
And in the middle with myrtle bound,
  High stood the archon king;
And beside him stood a milk-white bull,
  That never had known the yoke,
And waited now with patient neck,
  The sacrificing stroke.
Then, with a heaven-directed gaze,
  And hands uplifted high,
The high priest of Eleusis prayed
  To Jove that rules the sky:

"O mighty Jove! who sway'st above,
   As kings are strong below,
To him that ruled our Attic land
   From thee shall honour flow.
The bull we slay, the stone we lay
   To Ægeus' son divine,
But vain the toil unless thy smile
   May bless the rising shrine!"
He spoke, and straight with patient neck
   The bull received the stroke;
With gilded horn it smote the ground,
   And thus the high priest spoke:
"As humbled low beneath the blow
   The huge bull quivering falls,
So smite thou him, great Jove, whose hand
   Shall harm these rising walls!"
Then came the master-builder wise
   The corner-stone to lay,
And thus before the listening crowd
   With solemn voice doth say:
"This stable-pillared shrine secure
   While Athens stands shall stand,

And the frequent oar shall beat the shore
   Of the godlike Attic land!"
And while the corner-stone he lays
   With weighty pomp decorous,
Upswells the crowning hymn of praise
   From the mellow-throated chorus.

CHORUS OF ALL THE PEOPLE.

1.

Famous is Thebes, by thy birth made immortal,
   Son of Alcmena, whose bravery won
A place with the gods when Olympus' wide portal
   Flew open to welcome Jove's club-bearing son.
He griped the fierce lion with arm strong and pliant;
The oxen he stole from the three-bodied giant,
   Where the sun has his westering bed;
The snake hundred-headed to death he devoted,
From Hades he dragged the grim hound triple-
     throated,
   Whose bark splits the realm of the dead.

K

Through labours enorm
His conquering form
Pressed on with unsleeping endeavour,
Till wrapt in pure flame
He rose without blame
To the throne of his father for ever.

2.

Son of Alcmena, thy brother in danger
    Was Theseus, the pride of the old Attic land:
Nor he to thine honour might long be a stranger;
    Jove claimed him to swell the Olympian band.
The mountain centaurs, the shaggy assaulters
Of women he tamed: and from Attica's altars
    He drave the fierce Amazons far.
His arm still was raised for the poor and un-
        friended,
The reign of rude force by his strong will was
        ended,
    And law was the watchword of war.

And now at the board
Where Jove is the lord
He sits with the son of Alcmena;
And looks from the sky
With a joy-beaming eye
On the temple and town of Athena.

THE FEAST OF PALLAS ATHENA.[9]

Παλλάδος ἐν πόλει
τᾶς καλλιδίφρου τ' Ἀθαναίας
ἐν κροκέῳ πέπλῳ
ζεύξομαι ἄρματι πώλους,
ἐν δαιδαλέαισι
ποικίλλουσ' ἀνθοκρόκοισι πήναις,
ἢ Τιτάνων γενεὰν,
τὰν Ζεὺς ἀμφιπύρῳ
κοιμίζει φλογμῷ Κρονίδας ;— EURIPIDES.

"PRAISE to Pallas, virgin Pallas, Jove-born Pallas,
    praise to thee !
Thou dost crown with grace the worthy, thou
    dost gird with strength the free !
Mighty Jove unmothered bore thee; when the
    Highest throbbed with pain

Thou didst leap, an armèd maiden, perfect from
    his procreant brain.

From the strongest strong thou camest, from the
    wisest god most wise,

Piercing through each cloudiest error with thy
    clear cerulean eyes.

Thou dost wield the Thunderer's thunder with thy
    strong-compelling spear;

Where thou lookest stands the opposer powerless
    with the palsied fear;

Where thy father's shield thou shakest, fringed
    with snakes, what man may bear

All their bristling terror, who the trunkless Gor-
    gon's stony glare?

Where with firm-set foot thou marchest, lawless-
    swelling murmurs cease;

Rebel thousands fall before thee, where by war
    thou pavest peace;

Jove alone in high Olympus, maid divine, is like
    to thee;

Thou dost crown with grace the worthy, thou dost
    gird with strength the free."

Thus the city rings with praises, rock to plain
    gives back the glee,

For the great feast of Athena Athens rings with
    revelry.

Nobly have the games been ordered, nobly were
    the vases won;

With a wreath of sacred olive Athens twines each
    conquering son;

Nobly have the swift torch-bearers in long lines a
    nimble band,

Like swift light upon the waters, winged the torch
    from hand to hand;

Nobly with their fervid wheels the rattling chariots
    turned the goal,

While in billows multitudinous far the rival
    plaudits roll;

Nobly have the stout athletes displayed the breadth
    of manly form,

In the strife of graceful mastery brandished well
    the brawny arm;

Nobly the clear-throated singer taught the stable-
    banded chorus

How to swell the notes of triumph, how to lift the
    wail sonorous :

And thy song, Aristogeiton, and Harmodius' patriot
    lay,

While their swords they wreathe with myrtle,
    thrills each freeman's heart to-day.

Now the last, the greatest honour of this pomp of
    many days,

Fills each eye with bright amazement, fills each
    heart with forward praise.

Lo ! it comes the fair procession : see, where flaunt-
    ing in the gale,

From the sacred ship of Pallas floats the golden-
    broidered sail !

'Tis the stole of chaste Athena sporting in the
    breezy air ;

Modest maids with pious labour wove the gown
    that she shall wear ;

Who is near may see the cunning of those fingers
    fine that wove,

On that sacred stole, the combat of the godless
    crew who strove

'Gainst the immortals. Warlike Pallas stood at
    the right hand of Jove,

Firm with reasoned calm resistance 'gainst the
    Titans blindly blustering.

On they come portentous-roaring, all their gusty
    legions mustering,

Breathing fire, and belching smoke, and shaking
    Earth with fits of fear,

Where their serpent-feet huge-twining, where their
    hundred hands appear.

Thrice from their rocky sockets firm the stiff and
    far-fanged roots they tore

Of the trees that huge Olympus on his shaggy
    bosom bore;

Thrice was Ossa piled on Pelion; and the mon-
    stered height uphove,

On its top, the rebel brood who dared defy the
    might of Jove.

With her father's thunder, Pallas, and with light-
    ning's scorching flare,

Hurled them thrice in fall precipitous through the
    dark-convolvèd air;

And in senseless rout confounded through the
 yawning gates of hell,
Stiff with stony stupefaction from the blue-eyed
 maid they fell.
'Neath the ocean's root she bound them, by fair
 Sicily's smoking shore,
There to sleep an aching sleep, with feverish dreams
 for evermore,—
Dreams that tell by pillared flame, reeking earth,
 and seething water,
Vain, how vain is witless force against great Jove's
 high-counselled daughter.
Such the story of the stole the gentle-handed
 maidens wove,
To adorn thine ancient image mighty seed of mighty
 Jove;
And in triumph now they bear it, and to pave the
 festal way
Wisely marshalled bands attendant march in beau-
 tiful array.
From the highlands, from the lowlands, from steep
 Sunium's sounding waves,

Came to join the pious convoy all the lovely, all
    the brave :

Ancient elders hoary-bearded in the solemn van
    we see,

Bearing high the wavy branches of the sacred olive-
    tree ;

Aged women with them banded ; well beseems the
    old to bear

Peaceful signs, with peaceful words to tame hot
    hands that rashly dare.

Them the graceful riders follow, firm-set men that
    scour the field,

With the spear the brazen - pointed, ´with the
    hollow-rounded shield.

Then the matrons, decent-vested, faithful to their
    husbands' bed,

And the stranger women bearing water-pitchers on
    their head.

Next the young men crowned with millet, march
    with light and gladsome foot,

Singing praises to the goddess with the players of
    the flute,

And the noble-blooded maidens of Cecropia's purest
    race,

Bearing baskets nicely stored with tools for use of
    holy place.

Marshalled thus, and trimly banded with sedately
    measured speed,

From the Ceramicus wending they the long proces-
    sion lead,

By the shrine of boon Demeter, by the old Pelasgic
    wall,

By the place where Pythian Phœbus rears his lofty
    pillared hall,

By the Pnyx, the people's platform, whence the
    word electric speeds,

Word that fires the patriot's heart, and nerves his
    arm to manly deeds.

Thence with gradual sweep ascending to Erectheus'
    rocky home,

To the shrine of high-perched Pallas, with their
    jubilant troops they come;

Then before the sacred doorstead, when the last had
    reached the goal,

They unfurl the floating glory of the rich and
 saffron stole.

To the inmost cell they bring it, where the sacred
 image lies,

On a couch with flowers bestrewn, of Pallas, with
 cerulean eyes;

And selectest hands invest her with the robe which
 virgins wove

For the maid that keeps the city, daughter of
 immortal Jove—

While within the pictured porch, and round the
 far-drawn colonnade,

Thus the sacred hymn was sounded to Cecropia's
 blue-eyed maid :

"Praise to Pallas, virgin Pallas, Jove-born Pallas,
 praise to thee !

Thou hast crowned with gold the worthy, thou
 has girt with strength the free;

Not like Mars in blood delighting, blind, impetu-
 ous, warreth she,

Lashing wild the waves of battle like the tempest-
 fretted sea;

But with clear and calm decision, and with holy-
    glowing heart,

She to shield the peaceful labourer, whirls the spear
    and wings the dart;

From the rock with old Erectheus where sublime
    the virgin dwells,

Right and law and stable order she with gracious
    force compels.

When the gods in consultation sate to fix the
    doubtful claim

If Athena or Poseidon should be sponsor to its
    fame,

With his three-pronged mace the sea-god proudly
    struck the pregnant ground,

And with sounding hoof four - footed forth the
    generous steed did bound.

Like Poseidon's waves mane-tossing it did spurn
    the Attic clay,

High its strength-clad neck uprearing, proudly
    snorting for the fray.

Laughed the gods with loud approval; but with
    look serene and clear

Smote the rock Jove's blue-eyed daughter with her
  fine celestial spear;

And in green and graceful beauty rose the gentle
  olive-tree.

Jeered the gods; but Jove the wisest gave the
  peaceful palm to thee.

Wield who will the imperious sceptre, hold the
  tribes of earth in awe,

By the sword that knows no mercy, by the con-
  queror's ruthless law,

Athens, thine a nobler triumph; to be wise and to
  be free,

And to star thy track with science, this thy Pallas
  gave to thee.

Every art that peace can cherish she hath marked
  out in her plan,

By thy ministry to smooth each rough and savage-
  minded man.

With the axe and with the chisel, with the needle
  pointed fine,

She hath made each firmest fabric, every nicest
  texture thine.

She to rib the stoutly-timbered, stable-masted ship
    hath taught thee,
And with wings of flaxen tissue spread to willing
    winds hath brought thee
Gainful to the wealth-producing harbours of the
    foodful earth.
In the earthly breast she planted lofty thoughts of
    heavenly birth;
She for use of holy worship shapely stones on
    stones hath laid,
Piled the pillared porch, and gently curved the
    sweeping colonnade.
She hath taught the curious limner how to trace
    with breathing lines
Every limber form that moveth, every shifting
    hue that shines;
Taught the cunning-handed sculptor how the cold
    stone to inspire
With pure thought's calm brooding sweetness,
    with the glow of deep desire.
Wisdom she gave to the poet; though the brightest
    fancies flit,

Pointless falls the numerous strophe, where wise
Pallas lends not wit.

Praise to Pallas, virgin Pallas, mighty Jove's thrice-
mighty daughter!

She hath writ her nation's record not in lines of
crimson slaughter.

She will make her people teachers of the wise in
many lands,

And their tongue shall ring sonorous where the
thinker's watch-tower stands;

And from age to age unending, and from rolling
sea to sea,

Whoso names wise Athen's sages, wise Athena,
nameth thee!"

ÆSCHYLUS.[10]

ἔφη δὲ Αἰσχύλος μειράκιον ὢν καθεύδειν ἐν ἀγρῷ
φυλάσσων σταφυλὰς, καὶ ὁι Διόνυσον ἐπιστάντα
κελεῦσαι τραγῳδίαν ποιεῖν· ὡς δὲ ἦν ἡμέρα (πείθεσθαι
γὰρ ἐθέλειν) ῥᾷστα ἤδη πειρώμενος ποιεῖν. — PAUSANIAS.

NEAR Eleusis' holy city,
By the sacred-winding way,
Where the pomp was yearly marshalled
On Demeter's festal day,
Sate a youth, the vineyard watching,
'Neath the moony welkin fair,
'Mid the rich and leafy greenness,
Gazing mutely through the air;
Sate and mused, high-vaulting fancies
Taming with devoutest fear;

L

Mingling thoughts of far adventure
With the peaceful goddess near.
While pure Phœbe high was wheeling,
Thus his lonely watch he kept,
O'er each dim conception brooding,
Till the musing watchman slept.
Through his soft sleep's dreamy rapture,
Festive notes in tinkling war
Thrilled his ear; his eye bright Bromius
High-borne in a tiger-car,
Smote with wonder.   Soft-limbed beauty
Shone in him divinely fair,
Swam his eye in wavy gambol,
Floated free his sun-bright hair;
Crimson-mantled health, not faintly,
O'er his rounded cheeks was spread,
Coolest ivy bound his temples,
Horns of strength rayed from his head.
Thus the blooming vine-god beauteous
Lighted on the grassy sod,
And, with keen-felt presence glowingly,
To the mortal spake the god :

"Son of Euphorion, from Olympus
Sent, I come with haste to thee
Not unworthy; thou my singer
And Apollo's bard shalt be.
I thy thoughts have known the deepest,
The strong love that stirs thy soul;
Thou shalt run, divinely strengthened,
To the glory-glittering goal.
Where the stable banded chorus
Voices Dionysus' praise,
Thou shalt lead their songs in triumph,
Through the curious-measured maze.
From the cloudy dim tradition
Thou shalt call the heroes old;
To thy great conception imaged,
Kings and gods thine art shall mould.
From old Homer's banquet nicely
Thou shalt cull the various feast;
And the king of men from Hades'
All-embracing hold released,
At thy call shall march to Argos,
At thy word retrace his path

Back to where false Clytemnestra
Stabs him in the treacherous bath.
Thou the son shalt arm with vengeance,
Till the blood-stained mother die;
At thy call the hell-hounds furious,
With a sense-confounding cry,
Shall pursue the mother-murderer,
O'er the land and o'er the sea,
Wan and weary, worn and wasted,
Till a god shall speak him free.
To the old Cadmean fortress,
Breathing breath of haughty war,
Thou shalt guide the host white-shielded,
In the dust-enveloped car.
Thou the haughty-hearted Titan,
That with bitter words did rail
'Gainst the thunderer, to the storm-swept,
Ice-ribbed, snow-capt crag shalt nail."
Thus with words of lofty promise,
To the mortal spake the god;
Thrilled him with his keen-felt presence,
Touched him with his pine-tipt rod,

And waked the dreamer. He, upstarting
From his sweet entrancement, saw
In thin air the god evanishing,
And he worshipped him with awe.
And he vowed to be his singer,
And he sang full many a lay,
With religious power deep-throated,
From that consecrating day.
And he kept the trust committed
To his ward with reverent care,
Voicing fearless inspiration,
That men felt a god was there;
Till, with ivy crowned victorious,
He was hailed by Attic throngs:
Time their high approval glorious
Through far-sounding halls prolongs.

MARATHON.

Λειμῶνα τόν ἐρόεντα Μαραθῶνος.—ARISTOPHANES.

I.

From Pentelicus' pine-clad height [11]
　　A voice of warning came,
That shook the silent autumn night
　　With fear to Media's name.
Pan from his Marathonian cave [12]
　　Sent screams of midnight terror,
And darkling horror curled the wave
　　On the broad sea's moonlit mirror.
　　　　Woe, Persia, woe! thou liest low, low!
　　　　　Let the golden palaces groan!
　　　　Ye mothers weep for sons that shall sleep
　　　　　In gore on Marathon!

II.

Where Indus and Hydaspes roll,
    Where treeless deserts glow,
Where Scythians roam beneath the pole,
    O'er fields of hardened snow,
The great Darius rules; and now,
    Thou little Greece, to thee
He comes; thou thin-soiled Athens, how
    Shalt thou dare to be free?
        There is a God that wields the rod
          Above: by Him alone
        The Greek shall be free, when the Mede
          shall flee
        In shame from Marathon.

III.

He comes; and o'er the bright Ægean,
    Where his masted army came,
The subject-isles uplift the pæan
    Of glory to his name.

Strong Naxos, strong Eretria yield ;
   His captains near the shore
Of Marathon's fair and fateful field,
   Where a tyrant marched before.[13]
      And a traitor guide, the sea beside,
        Now marks the land for his own,
      Where the marshes red shall soon be the
        bed
        Of the Mede in Marathon.

IV.

Who shall number the host of the Mede ?
   Their high-tiered galleys ride,
Like locust-bands with darkening speed,
   Across the groaning tide.
Who shall tell the many-hoofed tramp
   That shakes the dusty plain ?
Where the pride of his horse is the strength of his
     camp,
   Shall the Mede forget to gain ?

Oh fair is the pride of those turms as they
    ride,
To the eye of the morning shown !
But a god in the sky hath doomed them to lie
    In dust, on Marathon.

v.

Dauntless beside the sounding sea
    The Athenian men reveal
Their steady strength.   That they are free
    They know; and inly feel
Their high election, on that day,
    In foremost fight to stand,
And dash the enslaving yoke away,
    From all the Grecian land.
        Their praise shall sound the world around,
           Who shook the Persian throne,
        When the shout of the free travelled over
           the sea,
           From famous Marathon.

VI.

From dark Cithæron's sacred slope,
   The small Platæan band
Bring hearts, that swell with patriot hope,
   To wield a common brand
With Theseus' sons, at danger's gates;
   While spell-bound Sparta stands,
And for the pale moon's changes waits
   With stiff unkindly hands;
     And hath no share in the glory rare,
      That Athens shall make her own,
     When the long-haired Mede with fearful
      speed
     Falls back from Marathon.

VII.

"On, sons of the Greeks!" the war-cry rolls;
   "The land that gave you birth,
Your wives, and all the dearest souls
   That circle round each hearth;

The shrines upon a thousand hills,
　　The memory of your sires,
Nerve now with brass your resolute wills,
　　And fan your valorous fires!"
　　　　And on like a wave came the rush of the
　　　　　　brave—
　　　　　"Ye sons of the Greeks, on, on!"
　　　　And the Mede stept back from the eager
　　　　　　attack
　　　　　Of the Greek, in Marathon.

VIII.

Hear'st thou the rattling of spears on the right?
　　Seest thou the gleam in the sky?
The gods come to aid the Greeks in the fight,
　　And the favouring heroes are nigh.
The lion's hide I see in the sky,
　　And the knotted club so fell,
And kingly Theseus' conquering eye,
　　And Macaria, nymph of the well.[14]

Purely, purely the fount did flow,
   When the morn's first radiance shone;
But eve shall know the crimson flow
   Of its wave, by Marathon.

IX.

On, son of Cimon, bravely on!
   And Aristides just!
Your names have made the field your own,
   Your foes are in the dust!
The Lydian satrap spurs his steed,
   The Persian's bow is broken;
His purple pales; the vanquished Mede
   Beholds the angry token
      Of thundering Jove who rules above;
       And the bubbling marshes moan [15]
      With the trampled dead that have found
        their bed
      In gore, at Marathon.

X.

The ships have sailed from Marathon,
    On swift disaster's wings;
And an evil dream hath fetched a groan
    From the heart of the king of kings.
An eagle he saw, in the shades of night,
    With a dove that bloodily strove;
And the weak hath vanquished the strong in fight,
    The eagle hath fled from the dove.[16]
        Great Jove, that reigns in the starry plains,
           To the heart of the king hath shown,
        That the boastful parade of his pride was laid
           In dust, at Marathon.

XI.

But through Pentelicus' winding vales
    The hymn triumphal runs,
And high-shrined Athens proudly hails
    Her free-returning sons.

And Pallas, from her ancient rock,
 With her shield's refulgent round,
Blazes; her frequent worshippers flock,
 And high the pæans sound,
   How in deathless glory the famous story
    Shall on the winds be blown,
   That the long-haired Mede was driven with
    speed
    By the Greeks, from Marathon.

XII.

And Greece shall be a hallowed name,
 While the sun shall climb the pole,
And Marathon fan strong freedom's flame
 In many a pilgrim soul.
And o'er that mound where heroes sleep,[17]
 By the waste and reedy shore,
Full many a patriot eye shall weep,
 Till Time shall be no more.

And the bard shall brim with a holier hymn,
   When he stands by that mound alone,
And feel no shrine on earth more divine
   Than the dust of Marathon.

SALAMIS.[18]

'Ω κλεινὰ Σαλαμὶς σὺ μέν που
ναίεις ἁλίπλαγκτος, εὐδαίμων
πᾶσιν περίφαντος ἀεί.—Sophocles.

SEEST thou where, sublimely seated on a silver-
footed throne,
With a high tiara crested, belted with a jewelled
zone,
Sits the king of kings, and, looking from the rocky
mountain-side,
Scans with masted armies studded far the fair
Saronic tide?
Looks he not with high hope beaming? looks he
not with pride elate?
Seems he not a god, the Thunderer? and his words
are winged with fate.

He hath come from far Euphrates, and from Tigris'
    rushing tide,

To subdue the strength of Athens, to chastise the
    Spartan's pride :

He hath come with countless armies, gathered
    slowly from afar,

From the plain, and from the mountain, marshalled
    ranks of motley war;

From the land, and from the ocean, that the
    burdened billows groan,

That the air is choked with banners, which great
    Xerxes calls his own.

Soothly he hath nobly ridden, o'er the fair fields,
    o'er the waste,

As the Earth might bear the burden, with a
    weighty-footed haste;

He hath cut in twain the mountain, he hath bridged
    the rolling main,

He hath lashed the flood of Helle, bound the billow
    with a chain;

And the rivers shrink before him, and the sheeted
    lakes are dry,

From his burden-bearing oxen, and his hordes of
cavalry;

And the gates of Greece stand open; Ossa and
Olympus fail;

And the mountain-girt Æmonia spreads the many-
watered vale;

And her troops of famous horse, before the puissant
Persian's nod,

Flee; the death-defying Spartans prostrate lie be-
neath his rod,

Where with fleshy breast they walled thy famous
pass, Thermopylæ.

And the god that shakes Cithæron feared to block
his forceful way;

And the blue-eyed maid of Athens shook not then
her heavenly spear,

Rock-perched Pallas, when the tread of the high-
clambering foe was near;

And the sacred snake, huge-twining guardian of the
virgin shrine,

Where the honeyed cake was waiting, tasted not the
food divine;

Stood nor man nor god before him ; he hath scoured
    the Attic land,

Chased the valiant sons of Athens to a barren
    island's strand ;

He hath hedged them round with triremes, lines on
    lines of bristling war ;

He hath doomed the prey for capture ; he hath
    spread his meshes far ;

And he sits sublimely seated on a throne with pride
    elate,

To behold the victim fall beneath the sudden-
    swooping Fate.

Who may stand against his might ?—with thy thin
    slip of rocky coast,

Athens, wilt thou tell thy fifties 'gainst the thou-
    sands of his host ?

All the might of all the Orient, from the Ganges-
    watered Ind

To the isles that fringe the Ægean, 'gainst thy
    little state combined ;

Turbaned Persians, with gay panoply from the gold
    of distant mines,

Host immortal with their wives, and troops of
    spangled concubines;

Mitred Cissians, high-capped Sacae, and the As-
    syrian brazen-crested;

The high-booted Paphlagonian; the swart Indian
    cotton-vested;

Shaggy warriors, goatskin-mantled, from the dreary
    Caspian strand,

And the camel-mounted riders from the incense-
    bearing land,

Thracians fierce, with shouts Bacchantic, and more
    savage war-halloo;

Sacred Tmolus' sons, and Lydia's soft and silken-
    vested crew;

And the sons of hoariest Thebes, and sacerdotal
    Memphis, where

Gods, in brutish incarnation, bellow through the
    sacred air;

And the sun-scorched, painted Ethiop, with his
    huge-spanned bow of war,

And the woolly-headed Libyan, driving swift the
    scythèd car;
And the boatmen of the lowland, that, with fre-
    quent-beating oar,
Plough the pools where floats the lotus, by the fat
    Nile's peopled shore:
Such a crew he drives against thee. 'Neath the
    dusky-vested Night,
He hath ranged them to entrap thee.

              Now behold the glorious light,
Beaming broadly from the chariot of the silver-
    steeded day,
Shows revealed the triple barrier of his ships in
    close array,
Girdling in the coast of Ajax. Yet no wavering
    fear is there;
Firmly stands the line of Athens.

             Hark! their loud shouts split the air.
Not the expected note of terror, not the wild cry
    of despair;

Foolish Xerxes! 'tis the exultant power that swells
    strong manhood's breast;
'Tis the broadly-billowed pæan from the freemen of
    the West.

"Sons of the Greeks! now save your country!
    save your wives and children dear!
Save the sepulchres of your fathers! save the
    shrines of gods that hear
When the patriot prays! This day makes us free
    or slaves for ever!"
On they sail, with steady helming, sworn to die or
    to deliver.
Now they meet. Now beak on beak is furious
    dashed; and Sidon old
Drives her brazen-breasted triremes 'gainst the ships
    of Athens bold.
A moment equal; but the Athenian, in the des-
    perate-handed strife,
Wields, as patriots well may wield, a surer sword
    and sharper knife.

On he presses—close and closer; cloven booms
and shattered sails,

And the frequent-crashing oarage, mark the track
where he prevails.

Ocean seethes beneath his fury; and the hostile-
fretted flood

Yawns to drink the reeling Tyrian, and the floun-
dering Cyprian's blood.

Sobs the wave with drowned and drowning:
where the narrow channels flow,

Vain the strife with death two-handed, here the
water, there the foe.

Ship on ship is rudely clashed; for in the narrow
strait confined,

Room is none to use their numbers; and, with
strivings vain and blind,

Where they move they clog the movements of the
friend they hoped to aid,

Where they fight they help the battle of the foe
they should have stayed.

Vainly, with her Carian triremes, o'er the terror-
tangled scene

Artemisia rides the battle like an Amazonian
    queen;

All is reasonless confusion.   O'er the purple-stream-
    ing tide,

Helmless ships and shipless pilots struggle with the
    billows' pride

Vainly—for the west wind rising with harsh wing
    and savage roar

Drives the foundered and the drowning countless
    on the Colian shore.

And to crown such wreck and carnage, when the
    hottest fight was o'er,

Rode the Athenian galleys proudly to a rocky
    islet's shore,

Near to Salamis — there the king, to top the
    sure-deemed victory,

Susa's chiefest bloom had stationed; and in wait-
    ing there they lie

To help their conquering friends, and swell the
    hoped-for triumph.   Them the foe

Circle round with bristling beaks, and, where the
    billowy waters flow,

Blast them with the arrowy tempest, crush them
    with the huge-heaved rock,

Mow them down in rows defenceless, like the butch-
    ered bleating flock.

From his throne the monarch sees it, heap on heap
    of helpless slaughter,

With the life of Persia crimsoned far the fair
    Saronic water.

Rend thy robes, thou foolish Xerxes, rend the air
    with piteous cries !

On the rocky coast of Hellas gashed the pride of
    Persia lies !

Wake thee ! wake thee ! blinded Xerxes ! God
    hath found thee out at last ;

Snaps thy pride beneath His judgment, as the tree
    beneath the blast.

Haste thee ! haste thee ! speed thy couriers—Per-
    sian couriers travel lightly—

To declare thy stranded navy, and by cruel death
    unsightly

Dimmed thy glory. Hie thee! hie thee! hence
e'en by what way thou camest,

Dwarfed to whoso saw thee mightiest, and where
thou wert fiercest, tamest!

Hide thee, where blank Fear shall hunt thee, and,
more surely to undo thee,

Thirst and hunger where thou goest, brothered
demons, shall pursue thee.

Where Cithæron dear to Bromius nods his horror-
crested wood,

To the Phocian, to the Dorian, where Sperchcius
rolls his flood,

Through Æmonia steed-delighting, by Magnesia's
wave-lashed strand,

Through the hardy Macedonian's, through the
fierce-souled Thracian's land,

By the reedy Bolbe's waters, by the steep Pangæan
height,

By the stream of holy Strymon thou shalt spur
thy sleepless flight.

Frost and Fire shall league together, wrathful
Heaven to Earth respond,

Strong Poseidon with his trident break thy im-
pious vaunted bond;

Where he passed, with mouths uncounted eating
up the famished land,

Now a slender skiff shall ferry Xerxes to the Asian
strand.

Haste thee! haste thee! they are waiting by the
palace-gates for thee,

By the golden gates of Susa eager mourners wait
for thee;

Haste thee, where the guardian elders wait, a
hoary-bearded train;

They shall see their king, but never see the sons
they loved again.

Where thy weeping mother waits thee, queen
Atossa waits to see

Dire fulfilment of her troublous vision - haunted
sleep in thee.

She hath dreamt, and she shall see it, how an
Eagle cowed with awe

Gave his kingly crest to pluck before a puny
Falcon's claw.

Haste thee! where the mighty shade of great
    Darius through the gloom
Rises dread, to teach thee wisdom, couldst thou
    learn it, from the tomb.
There begin the sad rehearsal, and, while streaming
    tears are shed,
To the thousand tongues that ask thee, tell the
    myriads of the dead!
Blame the god that so deceived thee — for the
    mighty men that died
Blame all gods that be, but chiefly blame thyself,
    and thine own pride!
Drown thy sorrow with much wailing! beat thy
    breast, thy vesture rend,
Tear thy hair, and pluck thy beard — weep till
    thou hast no tears to spend;
Call the mourning women to thee! while they lift
    the Mysian wail,
Thou to Susa's sonless mothers pour the sorrow-
    streaming tale!

HERACLITUS.[19]

Λέγει που Ἡράκλειτος ὅτι πάντα χωρεῖ καὶ οὐδὲν
μένει, καὶ ποταμοῦ ῥοῇ ἀπεικάζων τὰ ὄντα λέγει ὡς
δὶς ἐς τὸν αὐτὸν ποταμὸν οὐκ ἂν ἐμβάιης.—PLATO.

At Ephesus, by Cäyster's flood,
    The son of Blyson sate,
And mused, in darkly thoughtful mood,
    On God, and man, and fate.
And as he looked on the sleepless torrent
    Rolling to the sea,
With a whirling, swirling, eddying current,
    Thus to himself spake he:
        Nothing to hold itself is strong;
          But all things, like a river,
        Roll along, and swirl along,
          And bubble along for ever.

The tender blade, whose eager seed
  Broke through the teeming plain,
Shall blossom bear, with fated speed
  And end in seed again.
And when Spring's plastic sunbeam warm
  Shall thaw the wintry snow,
Abroad shall leap the prisoned germ,
  And life from death shall grow.
     For nothing to hold itself is strong;
      But all things, like a river,
     Roll along, and swirl along,
      And bubble along for ever.

Life from death, and death from life,
  So round and round it goes,
A ceaseless self-provoking strife,
  That ever ebbs and flows.
Within, without, and round about,
  Sans end, and sans beginning;
My brain reels with the mystic rout
  Of things for ever spinning.

For nothing to hold itself is strong;
 But all things, like a river,
 Roll along, and swirl along,
  And bubble along for ever.

Like the clouds that scour the sky,
 In the sleepless-shifting weather,
I know not how, I ask not why,
 Our thoughts chase one another.
Foolish fancies fret my brain,
 And thoughts which men call clever—
Waking, sleeping, pleasure, pain,
 The same, but shifting ever.
  For nothing to hold itself is strong;
   But all things, like a river,
  Roll along, and swirl along,
   And bubble along for ever.

The giant-snouted mountains grey,
 That seem to scorn mutation,
And see, like shadows, fleet away
 Man's feeble generation;

Their brows, which tyrannous blasts assail,
    Their peaks, which lightnings shiver,
With ceaseless ruin fill the vale,
    And feed the flowing river.
        For nothing to hold itself is strong;
          But all things, like a river,
        Roll along, and swirl along,
          And bubble along for ever.

All things that be like water flow,—
    The type of life is water;
But Heat makes motion swift or slow;
    FIRE is the soul of WATER.
When Heat invades the stiffened stream,
    The icy bonds are riven;
When sunbeams pierce the flood, the steam
    Swells in light airs to heaven.
        For nothing to hold itself is strong;
          But all things, like a river,
        Roll along, and swirl along,
          And bubble along for ever.

Motion, motion, holy Force,
 And Fire, pure fount of motion,
This sleepless-whirling world's course
 Shall claim my heart's devotion !
So float each thing of mortal name,
 On tides of joy and sorrow,
Ever the same, and never the same,
 The sport of each to-morrow !
   For nothing to hold itself is strong ;
    But all things, like a river,
   Roll along, and swirl along,
    And bubble along for ever.

ANAXAGORAS.[20]

'Αναξαγόρας τοῖς ὅλοις πρῶτος οὐ τύχην, οὐδ' ἀνάγκην
διακοσμήσεως ἀρχὴν, ἀλλὰ νοῦν ἐπέστησε καθαρὸν καὶ
ἄκρατον, ἐμμεμιγμένον πᾶσι τοῖς ἄλλοις, ἀποκρίνοντα
τὰς ὁμοιομερίας.—PLUTARCH.

Slow rolls the year that makes the sour grape mellow,
Slow spreads the blade that weaves the matted sod;
Slow o'er the grey rock creeps the lichen yellow,
Slow finds man's wandering wit its way to God.
WATER, quoth Thales, is the first of things;
Nay, quoth Anaximander, to my sight
The primal thing must be the INFINITE;
Quoth Anaximenes, 'tis AIR that brings
Life to all living; nay, 'tis FIRE that goes,
Quoth Blyson's son, through everything that flows.
Fools! saith, at length, wise Anaxagoras,
CAUSE never dwelt in aught of sensuous kind;
Sole first and last of all that is, and was,
And yet shall be, in Heaven or Earth, is MIND.

POLEMO.[21]

'Αμὴν ἀμὴν λέγω σοι, ἐὰν μή τις γεννηθῇ ἄνωθεν,
οὐ δύναται ἰδεῖν τὴν βασιλείαν τοῦ Θεοῦ.—JOHN iii. 3.

Peregrinatus est hic in nequitiâ, non habitavit.
—VALERIUS MAXIMUS.

'TIS morn.   On Parnes, nurse of hardy pines,
  Gleams the new-started day,
And on Ægina's briny water shines
  The clear far-shimmering ray.

'Neath the old Attic rock white vapours creep;
  And on the dusty road,
O'er the meek army of his bleating sheep
  The shepherd wields his goad.

The city sleeps ; save where the market shows
    The first green-furnished stalls, ,
And from his lair of shelterless repose
    The squalid beggar crawls.

Who bursts into the peaceful street, with sound
    Of brawl, and wrangling fray,
Rushing with blushless stare and staggering bound,
    To greet the modest day ?

A band of revellers, with torn chaplets crowned ;
    And at their head I know
The rich man's son, for shameless vice renowned,
    Licentious Polemo.

Onward they reel, as whim may point the way ;
    But he, with firmer pace,
Who hath a will strong to assert its sway
    Even in the drunkard's place.

And whither now? Sometimes God leads a fool
　　To knock at wisdom's door;
And so the reveller rushes to the school
　　Where Plato's holy lore

Is taught by sage severe Xenocrates,
　　Who, at that early hour,
Mingled wise disputation with the breeze
　　That stirred the learnèd bower.

Amid the listening scholars Polemo
　　Sate down; and, from his place,
With impudent stare his strong contempt did show,
　　In the mild lecturer's face.

The teacher saw, nor stirred his soul serene,
　　That reveller to reprove,
But changed his theme, and, with unaltered mien,
　　More apt discourse he wove

Of temperance, purity, high self-control,
    Ideal harmonies fine,
And all that lifts man's doubtful-swaying soul
    From bestial to divine.

The scoffer heard; but soon, with softened stare
    And flinching look, confessed
How deep the preacher probed his heart; for there
    He felt a strange unrest.

And as the wise man, with the waxing theme,
    More grave and weighty grew,
With swelling doubts he felt his bosom teem,
    His flushed cheek paled its hue.

And from his head he plucked the violets blue;
    And, as the speaker woke
More fretful tempest in his breast, he drew
    His hand beneath his cloak;

And rose; and stood as one that fronts a foe;
    Then, with a sudden turn,
Sank; in a gushing flood the salt tears flow;
    And, with wild thoughts that burn,

He from the audience rushed. But not his soul
    From the new awe that found him
Might rush; but, with a tyrannous strong control,
    Missioned from God, it bound him,

And with his mutinous temper wrestled long,
    Till, like a lamb, he lay;
Then rose, like one with a new nature strong,
    To a new life that day;

And by the chaste and blue-eyed goddess sware
    That, from that sacred hour,
He the philosopher's sober garb should wear,
    And walk in learnèd bower:

And, as he sware, so lived, that not a breath
  Might his pure fame besmirch;
And taught by word, and mightier deed, till death;
  A saint in Plato's church.

NOTES.

Note 1, p. 17.

" *The blind Smyrnéan minstrel.*"

Homer.—Of all the cities which contended for the honour of having given birth to the great epic singer of Greece, Smyrna has the best claims. See Müller's ' History of Greek Literature ;' Lauer's ' Homerische Poesie ;' or my ' Homer,' vol. i., Dissertation III.

Note 2, p. 32.

" PROMETHEUS."

No character of primeval Greek tradition has been a greater favourite with modern poets than the hero of the well - known play of Æschylus. The common conception of him, however, made fashionable by Shelley and Byron, as the representative of freedom in contest with despotism, is quite modern ; and Goethe is nearer the depth of the old myth, when, in his beautiful lyric, he represents the Titan as the impersonation of that indefatigable endurance in man

which conquers the earth by skilful labour, in opposition to
and in despite of those terrible influences of the wild ele-
mental powers of Nature, which, to the Greek imagination,
were concentrated in the person of Jove. On the apparent
impiety of the position of Prometheus, as against the
Olympian, see my 'Horæ Hellenicæ.'

Note 3, p. 37.

"THE NAMING OF ATHENS."

The beautiful and significant local myth embodied in
this ballad conveys a grand lesson in political economy to
all nations who, in the pursuit of wealth by manufactures,
commerce, or otherwise, may be tempted to neglect the
fundamental interests of landed property, and the rights of
the honest food-producing labourers who till the soil. It
were well for modern Greece, at the present hour, if it could
be brought to understand, and practically to strive after, the
realisation of this great principle. A people consisting of
mere merchants, without any root in the native soil, can
never become a nation. The contest between Pallas and
Poseidon was represented on the posterior pediment of the
Parthenon.—Pausanias, i. 24, 5. The same struggle be-
tween the same adverse deities existed in *Troezene*, and was
wisely compromised.—Pausan., ii. 30, 6. Gerhard remarks
that in these contests of local gods with Neptune the sea-
god is generally the loser.—'Mythol.,' 633 ; C. O. Müller,
'Minerva Pol.,' p. 7. To the English people, as the conser-
vators of the Elgin Marbles, the whole subject possesses a
peculiar interest.

Note 4, p. 46.

"BELLEROPHON."

This famous Corinthian legend has also become, in a manner, the property of the British nation, by the labours of Sir Charles Fellowes, and the existence of a "Xanthian Chamber" in the British Museum. Ephyre is the old name for Corinth. That Minerva, the goddess of wisdom, should appear as the special protector of a homicide, will seem strange to no thinker; for in those wild days of imperfect and partial law, feuds were always arising, and murders everywhere committed, and Furies invoked and feared by persons of the most reputable character. The scenery of the pass of Tretus, as given in p. 48, will be found described in Colonel Mure's two admirable volumes, entitled 'A Tour in Greece;' also in Curtius' 'Peloponessus,' ii. 505. The purification from the guilt of manslaughter by blood of swine (p. 49) is according to the well-known tradition of the ancient poets. On Xanthus, its topography and antiquities, besides the works of Sir Charles Fellowes, the reader may consult the two volumes of travels in Lycia, by the late Professor Edward Forbes and Colonel Spratt.

Note 5, p. 78.

"IPHIGENIA."

This subject has been as great a favourite with modern poets as the Prometheus. Goethe's play of this name is, by many, and for very good reasons, accounted his masterpiece.

The sacrifice of the Argive princess, besides its general human interest, is a striking testimony to the fact, that even among the most cultivated peoples of the ancient world, human sacrifice prevailed at an early period of their history. There are certain principles in the human heart which, at a certain stage of civilisation, seem to make such a practice a sort of moral necessity. That this practice existed even in the most polished age of Athens in a modified form is certain — *vide* the dictionaries, *in voce* φαρμακός. The idea of the substitution of the stag by Diana, in order to save the virgin's life, and the conveyance of the destined victim of a bloody devotion to the barbarous service of a grim idol in the Crimea, was an afterthought—one of those beautiful lies with which the legendary lore of old Hellas is replete. Æschylus, as is well known, in his sublime description of the sacrifice, in the opening chorus of the Agamemnon, altogether disregards the posterior fiction. How closely I have followed this great master in the closing stanzas of the ballad, will be obvious to the scholar. To have attempted originality after such a precedent would have been to insure failure.

Note 6, p. 88.

"Wail of an Idol."

In this lyric I have endeavoured to represent the very stupid and comfortless doctrine of the Greeks with regard to the state of human souls after death. The Greeks believed in a heaven and a hell, but only for the few : heaven for the very good, and hell for the very bad ; but the shades of the millions of common mortals were left floating about in a lethargic, inane sort of Limbo, not at all enviable. On this subject there is an excellent essay by Archbishop Whately, in his discourses on some characteristic points of Christianity. The reader may also consult my essay on the Theology of Homer, Proposition xix. in the 'Horæ Hellenicæ.'

Note 7, p. 95.

"ARIADNE."

This most beautiful legend of the Dionysiac series embodies a principle more Christian than Hellenic, but which belongs so essentially to the moral nature of man, that it is not possible for any religious mythology altogether to exclude it: the principle that I mean may be called *the consecration of sorrow*. Christian legends containing this moral, of which the number is very great, always represent suffering as the road to glory, and the cave of despair as the propylæa of the temple of bliss. The Hellenic legend has been a favourite subject with modern painters and sculptors; and the travelled reader will scarcely require to be told that the concluding part of this ballad is only a verbal paraphrase of the well-known statue of Ariadne by Dannecker, exhibited as one of the lions of Frankfort.

Note 8, p. 125.

"THESEUS."

The name of Theseus in early Attic civil history has the same significance as that of the bishop of Rome in the early history of the Christian Church. It signifies that unification of social aggregates, under a central directing power, which constitutes a state or a church ; and such a unity in the common course of things is personal in its rise and monarchical in its character. It comes into birth by the influence of a dominant personality, and continues personal in its form till a more ripe state of society invites the experiment of a form of social organism more or less democratic. The bringing of the bones of Theseus from the island of Scyros to his native city, afforded the Athenians an opportunity of publicly recognising this significant position of their great local hero in the history of their society ; and of this recognition the temple of Theseus, the best preserved of all Athenian monuments, presents a visible testimony to the eye of the intelligent traveller at the present day. The reader who may be anxious to verify the allusions in the text, may consult Plutarch's ' Lives of Theseus and Cimon,' and the article "Pyanepsion" in Dr Smith's 'Dictionary of Classical Antiquities.'

Note 9, p. 148.

"The Feast of Pallas Athena."

The possessors of the Elgin Marbles scarcely require to be reminded that the Athenians celebrated the supremacy of their great national goddess in a great feast recurring at stated intervals, called the "Panathenæa." The principal materials from which the present ballad was composed will be found in Dr Smith's Dictionary under that word. And the procession described in the text is the same as that which appears on the well-known frieze of the Elgin Marbles, which are as familiar to every person of cultivated taste as the Madonnas of Raphael or the portraits of Rembrandt.

Note 10, p. 161.

" ÆSCHYLUS."

The occupation of watching the vineyards, in which the father of tragedy is here represented as engaged, when the first inspiration came to his soul by the Epiphany of the patron god of the "goat song," is often alluded to by ancient writers. — See Song of Solomon, i. 6.   The works of the poet alluded to in the ballad are the 'Agamemnon,' the 'Choephorœ,' the 'Furies,' the 'Seven against Thebes,' and the 'Prometheus Bound,' being five out of the seven extant. The allusion to Homer in p. 163 is with reference to a well-known saying of the bard, reported by Athenæus (viii. p. 348), that his numerous tragedies were only "slices from the great banquet of Homeric dainties."

Note 11, p. 166.

" Pentelicus' pine-clad height."

Pentelicus overhangs the south side of the plain of Marathon, separating it from the great Attic plain.   Those who have seen the beautiful Bay of Brodick, in the island of Arran, have seen Marathon on a small scale, except that Goat Fell, which represents Pentelicus, is on the north. On the south, or Athenian side, this famous mountain is sufficiently bare, but towards Marathon it is richly wooded; and the direct road from the village of Vrana to the valley of the Cephissus, over the north-west shoulder of the mountain, is one of the wildest and most picturesque passes in Greece.

Note 12, p. 166.

"Pan's Marathonian cave."

Pan played a somewhat prominent part in the great Persian war (Herodotus, vi. 105). He had a famous cave near Marathon (Pausan., i. 32), which archæologists have idly endeavoured to identify.

Note 13, p. 168.

" A tyrant marched before."

Darius was led by Hippias, who was familiar with this approach to Attica, having come this way with his father Pisistratus, when that tyrant established himself in the sovereignty of Attica for the last time.

Note 14, p. 171.

" Macaria, nymph of the well."

Hercules was the patron saint, to use modern language, of Marathon; and, where the Athenians conquered, Theseus could not be absent. These two heroes, therefore, were represented in the picture of the battle of Marathon in the painted Stoa (Pausan., i. 15; Plutarch—Theseus, 35). The fountain of Macaria, the daughter of Hercules and Deianeira, is mentioned by Pausanias (i. c. 32) as being on ac field of Marathon; and sure enough there is a well on the ,oad from Marathon to Rhamnus, near the north end of the plain, which Mr Finlay is willing to baptise with the name of the old classical nymph.

Note 15, p. 172.

" The bubbling marshes moan."

There are two extensive marshes, mostly overgrown with great reeds, one at each end of the field. The Persians, of course, were driven back into the marsh at the north end. s was represented in the painting on the Stoa.

Note 16, p. 173.

" The eagle hath fled from the dove."

The idea here is taken from Atossa's dream, in 'The Per-.ians' of Æschylus, mentioned in the previous ballad.

Note 17, p. 174.

" That mound where heroes sleep."

The famous mound in the middle of the battle-field, men - tioned by Pausanias, and described by all modern travellers.

Note 18, p. 176.

"SALAMIS."

In this ballad an attempt has been made to unite the descriptions of this great naval combat, given by Herodotus and Æschylus. The tragic writer was a soldier, and present at the battle, which circumstance makes his testimony, as given in 'The Persians,' peculiarly valuable. The concluding part of the ballad is a sort of lyrical epitome of that very singular, and in some respects altogether unique, remnant of the lost riches of tragic art in Athens.

Note 19, p. 189.

"HERACLITUS."

The striking contrast between rest and motion, permanence and mutability, eternity and time, being and becoming, which the phenomena of the universe present, could not fail to occupy, at a very early period, the subtle minds of the Greek speculators. In Heraclitus the more sensuous of these two aspects, or the external of the two factors, was raised into a watchword of his philosophy, in the maxim πάντα ῥεῖ; a view of things which, when stated absolutely and unqualified by the recognition of the opposite view springing from the principle of λόγος or νοῦς, leads directly to universal scepticism, and shallow sophistry of that kind which became afterwards so rank in Athens, and required all the diligence of such master-workmen as Socrates and Plato to weed it out. Modern Sensationalism, issuing from the loose inductions of Locke, has produced similar results, for which a Scotsman does not require to seek far.

Note 20, p. 194.

"ANAXAGORAS."

Though Socrates, in several places of Plato, expresses his dissatisfaction with the doctrine of νοῦς, as taught by Anaxagoras, the friend of Pericles, there can be no doubt that, in comparison with those who preceded him, the philosopher of Clazomenæ is fully entitled to the proud position given him by Aristotle, and which has been asserted in the present sonnet.

Note 21, p. 195.

"POLEMO."

The very remarkable history of the conversion of this father of the old Academy, from a licentious to a saintly life, will be found in Valerius Maximus, lib. vi. c. 9, and in Diogenes Laertius. Those who wish to know where the Christian Church was before Christ (as we talk of "Reformers before the Reformation"), must search in the lives of the old Greek philosophers, who were not mere talkers and speculators, but men of character and action, and exhibiting in many cases a self-control and a self-denial, and a plain godly simplicity of life, which might shame not a few British Christians, who contrive in a very questionable sort of way to unite the worship of God with that of Mammon. A Socrates and a Polemo would certainly not have sinned after this fashion.